THE QUARTER HORSE IS GOOD ENOUGH FOR ME

*

WILL
ROGERS

COLONIAL RACE HORSE

An etching of a colonial race horse, published in the early 1800's, the type found bearing the following initials by his name, C. A. Q. H., meaning Celebrated American Quarter Horse. These were the foundation of the modern day Quarter Horse, and one of the reasons some American Thoroughbreds are not accepted as pure bred in England.

THE
Quarter Horse

A varied assortment of historical articles, equine biographies and characteristics, sketches of horsemen and other lore, all pertaining to the Quarter Horse.

PENNED UP
BY BOB DENHARDT

Foreword by JIM JENNINGS

TEXAS A&M UNIVERSITY PRESS
COLLEGE STATION

First published by the American Quarter Horse Association, 1941

Copyright 1941 by Bob Denhardt
Copyright © 1982 by Bob Denhardt
All rights reserved

Manufactured in the United States of America

First Paperback Edition
ISBN 1-58544-047-7

TO

Jack, Lee and Jim

FOREWORD

To say that Bob Denhardt wrote this book isn't exactly true. Bob Denhardt did write more of it than anyone else, and he compiled all the other parts to make up a volume of what once was more stories about Quarter Horses than had ever been published under one cover.

The Quarter Horse was the first book ever published about the then new breed. The original printing came out in 1941, just one year after the formation of the American Quarter Horse Association. No one had a better right to put together this book than did Bob Denhardt; the formation of that association was his idea. He worked out its constitution and by-laws and was its first executive secretary.

Denhardt's first introduction to the Quarter Horse was in 1937, when he became friends with author J. Frank Dobie. Denhardt was doing graduate work at the University of California at Berkeley, and had written some articles for *The Western Horseman*. Dobie, seeing the young man's interest in horses and riding, told him about some tough little horses down in Texas, horses that could sure enough work a cow and were plenty fast. He said they were called Steel Dusts.

Later that same year, Denhardt was offered a teaching position at the Agricultural and Mechanical College of Texas and found himself right in the middle of Steel Dust country. What ended as the formation of the American Quarter Horse Association began as a search for those legendary Steel Dust horses.

In the beginning, Denhardt wasn't even sure that there was a horse called Steel Dust, but he finally discovered that Peter McCue, through Dan Tucker, traced back to that stallion. Then, as he traveled throughout the Southwest, visiting ranches in Texas, New Mexico, Colorado, and Arizona, he found that those who owned descendants of Steel Dust held the horse in great esteem. But he also discovered that many horses called Steel Dusts did not trace back to that horse at all. They were of a common type, however, and were called by the name for lack of another.

Denhardt found this type of horse throughout the Southwest. He also discovered that nearly all the better Steel Dust stallions went back to just a few sires—horses like Traveler, Peter McCue, Weatherford Joe Bailey, and Old Fred. However, the breeders themselves, for the most part, did not know of the existence of each other and their similar horses. No one was keeping records, and no one before Denhardt had ever been interested enough to travel around and accumulate this information. As Denhardt said, "The better, older breeders knew the breeding of their own sires' top lines, but they had no way to know that similar blood was being used by other breeders in other states."

Denhardt continued to interview the top breeders of the time —men like George Clegg, Ott Adams, and Jack Casement—and found that all their horses went back to one of eight or nine key stallions. It was with this in mind that Denhardt began to think of a stud book for those horses, and in 1939 he wrote all the ranchers he had been visiting over the past couple of years, inviting them to a meeting. Unfortunately, not enough showed up.

He tried again in 1940 and that time was successful. Stock was sold, and a corporation called the American Quarter Horse Association was formed. In 1982 the Association tried to repay him for his efforts. Bob Denhardt became one of the first inductees into the American Quarter Horse Hall of Fame.

Jim Jennings
Assistant Editor and
Editorial Director
The Quarter Horse Journal

PREFACE

IN 1937 while the author was in California, Paul Albert, Editor of the Western Horseman *asked for an article on the Quarter Horse. He said that to the average horseman outside of Texas they were but rumors of an ideal horse. Whenever any horse was outstanding he would be called a Quarter Horse.*

While the author was writing this article he looked for some stories on the Quarter Horse and for the first time he realized just how scattered and sparse they really were. The writings of Dan D. Casement and William Anson constituted the principal references for the article finally submitted, called "The Quarter Horse, Then and Now." While gathering the material for this article the idea of some day corralling and publishing the best of the Quarter Horse literature presented itself to the author. Since the appearance of that story, more material has been uncovered and several more articles written. The American Quarter Horse Association has been organized, which also has helped create a demand for information. The author hopes this roundup will in some ways answer the demand for reading material on the Quarter Horse.

Dan D. Casement is really responsible for the Introduction. When proof-reading his article, "Concho Colonel, His Life and Times," although the author had read it at least ten times before, he became so stirred up that it no longer seemed right to let this great assembly go without some comments about the articles. Therefore in the Introduction is found an idea of the content and the editor's opinion of the article.

A few liberties have been taken by the editor with the various stories contained in this volume. The titles have been changed in some cases for two reasons. First, when originally published they just about had to mention Quarter Horses in the title so that the readers could tell what the article was about. In this collection, which is limited to Quarter Horse items, this was not necessary. Secondly, by leaving out the reference to Quarter Horse in some of the titles they could be shortened or changed to give them more color. Another liberty taken was in omitting in some cases the first part of the article, or the last part. This was done particularly where references were made to another article carried in the original magazine which is not of interest to the reader of this volume. In the Authors Index the correct title and place of publication is given. Footnotes were also deleted; if they were factual they were put in the text in parentheses; if references, they were entirely omitted.

This book should provide a starting place for future writers and Quarter Horse enthusiasts. Here in one group are the articles of a rapidly disappearing generation. All of them are interesting. After supper when the pipes are lit and the fire is burning, it is real sport to tell how Chunky Bill could follow a cow or how Coal Oil Johnny would squat and wait with pointed ears for the starting signal, and then jump twenty-four feet and come out like a hoop rolling to beat his opponent. To recount past exploits is helpful, but the future is of more immediate concern. We need to know more about the Quarter Horse. Where and why does he differ from other horses? Romance around the fire in the evening telling of inherent cow sense and natural ability to start and stop, and other pat phrases glibly repeated with no intention of offering definite proof are fine, but any mongrel might have these. Where and why, scientifically proven, has the Quarter Horse certain different and better characteristics? This can be shown. First we must find out physiologically wherein he differs from other horses, and then find out just why this helps him be a better animal for his particular utility. We need to find out his weaknesses, for he has them, and eliminate them wherever possible. When all this is done we who love these chunky ponies can say without the present sense of futility, even to owners of other breeds—the Quarter Horse is the greatest cow horse and short distance race horse ever to look through a bridle.

Bob Denhardt.

Texas A. & M.
College Station, Texas
June 30, 1941

CONTENTS

PAGE

Introduction - - - - - - - - - - Bob Denhardt - xv

PERSONAL OBSERVATIONS AND REMINISCENCES

Concho Colonel, His Life and Times - -	Dan D. Casement	3
He Was Called Billy - - - - - - -	H. T. Fletcher -	21
Master of Two Trades - - - - - - -	Jack S. Casement	26
Cold Deck and Short Races - - - - -	Gene M. Moses -	33
I Do Not Like Him - - - - - - -	Grove Cullum -	38
I Object - - - - - - - - - - -	Jack S. Casement	44
"Short-Horse" Men - - - - - - - -	Bob Denhardt -	51

ONE HORSE OR FAMILY

Billy Horses and Steel Dust - - - - -	J. Frank Dobie -	63
The South Texas Quarter Horse - - -	Bob Denhardt -	68
New Light on Old Steel Dust - - - -	Bob Denhardt -	76
Peter McCue, Wonder Horse - - - -	Bob Denhardt -	86
The Great Little Horse Billy - - - -	Helen Michaelis -	96

QUARTER HORSE HISTORY

The Oldest Distinct Breed - - - - -	William Anson -	109
Quarter-of-a-Mile Running Horses - - -	William Anson -	119
Importance of Racing and the Remount	Grove Cullum -	124
"Short-Horses" - - - - - - - - -	Bob Denhardt -	135
The Quarter Horse, A History - - - -	Bob Denhardt -	141

CONTENTS (Continued)

PAGE

The Southwestern Cow Horse - - - - Bob Denhardt - 152
The Colonial Quarter Horse - - - - - *J. Goodwin Hall* 159
The Quarter Horse in Mexico - - - - *Helen Michaelis* - 181

UTILITY, PERFORMANCE, CHARACTERISTICS

Explanation for Speed - - - - - - - Bob Denhardt - 189
Is the Quarter Horse a Thoroughbred? - Bob Denhardt - 196
The Social Significance - - - - - - *Dan D. and Jack S. Casement* 204
Worth His Salt - - - - - - - - - *Albert Hand* - - 210
Losin' One's Shirt - - - - - - - - *Wayne Gard* - - 216

Authors Index Containing Original Title and Place of
 Publication - - - - - - - - - - - - - - - 226
General Index - - - - - - - - - - - - - - 228

ILLUSTRATIONS

Colonial Race Horse		Frontispiece
Balleymooney		Facing page 6
Red Dog		" " 6
Little Steve		" " 7
Dexter in Action		" " 7
Lobo in Action		" " 22
Billy Byrne		" " 22
George Clegg		" " 23
Tom Benear		" " 23
Del Rio Joe		" " 38
Lucky Strike		" " 39
Squaw		" " 39
Lobo		" " 54
Little Joe, Jr.		" " 54
Rialto		" " 55
Joe Bailey of Gonzales		" " 55
Peter McCue		" " 70
Peter McCue		" " 71
Golden Chief		" " 86
Harmon Baker		" " 86
Coliseum in Fort Worth		" " 87
Dan Tucker		" " 87
Rocky Mountain Tom		" " 87
Tony		" " 102
Joe Hancock		" " 102

xiii

ILLUSTRATIONS *(Continued)*

Whimpy	Facing page 103
Thoroughbred Whirlaway	" " 118
Quarter Horse Tony	" " 118
Sir Archy	" " 119
Quarter Race in Mexico	" " 119
White Stockings	" " 134
Lady Speck and Don Manners	" " 134
Brown Jug	" " 135
Sam Jones	" " 135
Dun Hancock	" " 166
Jimmie Allred	" " 166
Bob Crosby Roping	" " 167
Dutch McCue	" " 167
Quarter Horse Men	" " 182
Pancho	" " 182
Margie	" " 183
Fannie	" " 183
Frosty	" " 198
Quarter Horse Officials	" " 198
Young Cold Deck	" " 199
Little Joe III	" " 199

☆   ☆   ☆   ☆   ☆   ☆

INTRODUCTION

By BOB DENHARDT

IT IS DOUBTFUL whether a better article on Quarter Horses has been written than Dan D. Casement's article "Concho Colonel, His Life and Times." Certainly there are none this editor has enjoyed more. Dan Casement comes from a line of public-spirited frontiersmen, and he did not desert the cause. Underneath his public spirit lies that same love of horses and ranch life that caused his father to prove up a homestead in the Unaweep Canyon of Colorado, and it is in this connection, as a lover, user, and evaluater of horse flesh that we find him writing this article, telling and reflecting a life full of experience. A horse to Dan Casement is not a mechanical unit designed solely for utility, he is also flesh and blood, to be loved and respected. Much of Dan Casement's philosophy can be seen in the following quotation: "They know that the most specific antidote to this short shift machine age is a predawn till after dusk set in a saddle. They know that organized Q. H. husbandry, if run right, will yield as big a crop of human values as horse flesh."

The article by H. T. Fletcher is one of the most important Quarter Horse documents because of the author's knowledge and description of Billy. He states, and there is no particular reason for questioning, that a neighbor of his knew Billy and his owner well and described them to him. His description tallies today with our idea of a real Quarter Horse. It would seem logical to believe his first hand account, written two decades ago, more than some of the hand-me-down hearsays of today. His quotation from a Crawford Sykes letter regarding Arch Oldham, Billy and Rondo constitutes some of the most authentic material we have. Clay McGonigle's record of 19 seconds for the steer roping which he quotes has been broken by Carl Arnold while engaged in a roping match with Bob Crosby at Carlsbad, New Mexico. (See illustration, facing page 167.) In a return engagement held at Roswell, New Mexico, Arnold succeeded in obtaining the title "World's Champion Steer Roper" when Crosby's great Quarter Horse, June Bug, who is generally conceded to be the greatest of all roping horses, fell with the title holder and he was unable to continue the contest. Crosby set the best time in that contest, however, roping and tying a steer in 19.4 seconds.

The third article, "Master of Two Trades," was written by Dan Casement's son, Jack. Jack Casement, after a well rounded early life which included an Eastern name college and cow punching in West Texas, is today capably managing the Casement "triangle bar" ranch in the Unaweep Canyon of Colorado, the third Casement in direct line to operate this spread. It would be hard to find two men as differently alike as Dan and Jack Casement. Jack is sharp, where Dan would be delicate; Jack is cynical, where Dan would be deferential; he is dogmatic, where his father would be prudent, but he is a Quarter Horse man with horse sense, and so is his father. His brilliant mind and his keen sense of humor make his writings more than enjoyable, and to the point. Like his father, he feels a horse is an individual with almost as much character and as much personality as many people.

Gene Moses, who wrote "Cold Deck and Short Races," did not know that Cold Deck left a son besides Big and Little Mike, the one that Coke Blake used as foundation for the Blake horse. However, his article gives us some of the best material available on Cold Deck. Moses said that a Mike horse was living in Lamar, Missouri, in 1924, but he looked like a plow horse. What Mr. Moses probably did not realize was that some Quarter Horses weigh up to nearly 1,500 pounds. Peter McCue weighed 1,440 and ran the quarter in 21 seconds, according to reports. Most of his criticisms are equally true of some Thoroughbreds. It is interesting to note how carefully he states that he is *not* comparing Quarter Horses with Thoroughbreds. One might wonder which group he was trying to appease.

"I Do Not Like Him," an article by Grove Cullum, should perhaps have been left out of this collection of articles, supposedly in favor of Quarter Horses. However, Cullum's article has its place. To understand it you must understand the man. He has spent the best years of his life where most every influence he officially contacted ceaselessly chanted the ultimate perfection of the Thoroughbred. The major, for that he is, could not be impartial; and since he could not be, and since he is a real horseman, he has picked out the most common faults in our average Quarter Horse, and given them to us straight from the shoulder. Quarter Horses do have faults, and so would any other horse that was crossed indiscriminately with every other member of his breed. The Studbook was established to eliminate faulty blood from the Quarter Horse. It might be added that printed immediately after Cullum's article is an answer which appeared in the same magazine soon after Cullum's article. Its tart comment on Cullum's article leaves no doubt the author is a Quarter Horse man, and the style is the style of Jack Casement.

It has been the author's good fortune to have known some of the truly great Quarter Horse men. The article entitled "Short-Horse Men" was written from the notes taken by the author when he was visiting their home range. There are more yet to be written about. Men in many ways just as important. For example take George Clegg, Coke Roberds, Dan Casement or Jim Minnick. These men made such names famous as Little Joe, Old Fred, Balleymooney, and Rainy Day. Then, too, there is rapidly arising another generation, composed of men like Raymond Dickson, Jack Casement, Jack Hutchins, Bob Kleberg, Ronald Mason, Maxie Michaelis, Ed Springer, Lee Underwood, Bill Warren, and more. They, too, deserve notice. The author hopes the time will come when he will have the opportunity to give all of these men their due. The Quarter Horse owes them much.

One Horse or Family

J. Frank Dobie's article, "Billy Horses and Steel Dust," was one of the earliest modern attempts to gather together the various stories of Billy and Steel Dust and to weave them into a coherent pattern. He was never able to tell if Steel Dusts and Billys were the same. Denhardt's article on "The South Texas Quarter Horse" was written in part as an answer to this question, showing how they both traced back to the same lines.

Since this article on the Billy Horse was written by Denhardt, new material has shown that Quarter Horse blood lines can be narrowed down to two principal families, Steel Dust and Shilo. Traveller today seems less important. Also further research has shown that Jim Ned *was* sired by Pancho, who was by Old Billy. If this article has any particular value, it is that it gathers together the scattered fragments and presents them in one unified story.

"New Light on Old Steel Dust" was written after the author had stumbled upon an old pedigree of Dan Tucker while in Colorado during a trip in the summer of 1939, with Lee Underwood of Wichita Falls, Texas. A visit was made to the man who last owned Peter McCue, Coke T. Roberds. During the conversation that followed, Mr. Roberds went to look for some pictures and papers and came up with the stud advertisement which had the first written record of Steel Dust's pedigree that the author had found. (See illustration, facing page 87.) Outside of this material, most of the article is a rehash of articles by Dan Casement and J. S. Shelton.

When a person realizes how many stories locate Steel Dust in the Denton area, and give the names of Batchler, Ellis, Bailes and Perry as those interested, there seems no reason to doubt that this was the Texas home of Steel Dust, and that these were the men connected with him.

Denying the existence of Steel Dust because he left no written record is about like denying the existence of Sam Bass—he couldn't write either.

The article on "Peter McCue" was one of the first the author wrote, and at that time, even though it was only a few years ago, much of the information we now have was lacking. The conclusions then drawn, however, have fortunately been proven true. Tad Moses, editor of the greatest "cow-sheet" ever published, *The Cattleman,* is indirectly responsible for this article.

Trammell and Newman were as good as any horse breeders that have lived in Texas. Locating at Sweetwater, they soon were turning out "Short-Horses" that were setting track records with great persistency. About this time the tracks were closed to all horses that were not registered Thoroughbreds. Two of Trammell's greatest sires were Quarter Horses, Barney Owens and Dan Tucker. They came from the celebrated Watkins family in Illinois. Besides Barney Owens and Dan Tucker, it might be mentioned, Trammell and Newman had a registered Thoroughbred stallion. Pan Zareta, Callise, Booger Red and many other names have made this Texas racing partnership world famous.

The most up-to-date article on the Billy Horse now is Helen Michaelis' article entitled "The Great Little Horse Billy." It is the best article written on the subject. With her natural enthusiasm and love for Quarter Horses, she has run down every lead and gotten together the pertinent facts. She has personally interviewed many individuals while traveling in several states, and, as a result, knows more about them than most any other living person.

Quarter Horse History

Part Three, the section dealing with Quarter Horse history, is the most repetitious of any of the sections. The reason for this is that to date we have had but one important historian of the Quarter Horse, namely, William Anson, of Christoval, Texas. The lead article is an article by Mr. Anson, which is entitled "The Oldest Distinct Breed." It is the best historical sketch of the Quarter Horse ever written, and in an indirect way is a good commentary on his own breeding operations. It is easy to see why he was one of the best breeders of Quarter Horses we have had. The historical articles by Casement, Cullum and Denhardt merely repeat and rewrite what old history William Anson gave in his articles. This, of course, will not hold true for all the detail, but for the most part is correct. This is probably the most finished and complete of his various articles which contain Quarter Horse history.

Uncle Billy Anson, as he was familiarly known by many of his friends, has an excellent article entitled "Quarter-of-a-Mile Running Horses." One of the most interesting parts of this article is that he says he talked to men who had known Bruce (first compiler of the Thoroughbred Studbook, 1832), and they said that he was an ardent admirer of the Quarter Horse. He also shows how many of our Thoroughbreds trace back to Quarter Horses, because Bruce, the first recognized compiler, entered horses in his book which had been recorded by Edgar, an earlier compiler, frankly as Quarter Horses. Another interesting point was his belief and partial proof that Justin Morgan was a Quarter Horse.

"Importance of Racing and the Remount," by Grove Cullum, represents one of the best summaries of the subject, in spite of his backhand thrusts at the Quarter Horse. There is one thing about this article of Cullum's, and that is he does not confine his criticism to the Quarter Horse, but broadens it out to include the Arab, the Morgan, the Standard Bred and the American Saddle Horse; in fact, all horses except his favorite, the Thoroughbred. There is one sentence that is of special interest. It is that the Thoroughbred can outrun the Quarter Horse from the length of a corn cob until they both starve to death. If anyone has a Thoroughhred of unquestioned breeding (i.e., having no Quarter Horse blood in the last few generations) who fancies he can outrun a Quarter Horse for any distance up to a quarter, and has plenty of money to post with a reputable concern, the editor believes a race could be arranged, and would be delighted to handle the details. Maybe some of those men who say a Thoroughbred can do everything better than any other horse will be interested in this proposition.

The article entitled "Short-Horses" is a heterogeneous group of facts, more or less interesting, and accumulated from many sources. "The Quarter Horse, A History," was written with the idea of summarizing the known history of the Quarter Horse, and to give to the public, who, to a large extent, is uninformed and unacquainted with the work of William Anson, a bird's-eye view of the development of the Quarter Horse to the present date. It was sent to *Country Life* in 1940 and was accepted. As this is being written, August, 1941, it still has not been published. The assumption is that Peter Vischer, the editor, will not mind it being printed here, as to date, it has never been returned as suggested, or published as desired.

J. Goodwin Hall became interested in the history of the Quarter Horse after the organization of the Quarter Horse Association. After reading the few articles available, he made several trips to New York and the Old South and purchased or borrowed all of the old books, such as Bruce, Edgar and Herbert, and with them he is working out the history as begun by Anson. This article on the Colonial Quarter Horse represents one of his first contributions, and he seems likely to be the man to take Anson's place as the best historian of the Quarter Horse.

Helen Michaelis has written an important article on "Quarter Horses in Mexico." One point which might have been brought out a little more was the fact that many Quarter Horses from the United States have found their way into Mexico. This was especially true between 1915 and 1925. Today Mexico is still taking them across the border in large numbers. It was only a few months ago that a friend of the editor's, one Sr. J. D. Raines, of Mexico City, took four of the best "short-horses" out of Texas and Louisiana. They were Ginger Rogers, White Stockings, Annabelle and Henry Star. Raines recently told the editor: "The racing of Quarter Horses in this country (Mexico) is second in importance to the number of races run in Texas. Personally I am in the mining business, but generally labeled as being for pleasure purposes, I have eight horses which are for matching in our races, as a rule in distances from 300 varas [275.58 yards] to 600 varas [551.16 yards]. I matched Ginger Rogers against the champion mare of Vera Cruz, called La Gaviota. I might add by means of wagers I myself was rewarded handsomely for beating this champion." The English is his, and no doubt he was. There is a picture of this race facing page 119. The picture of White Stockings, one of the Quarter mares purchased by Sr. Raines, appears facing page 134.

Utility, Performance, Characteristics

The fourth section of this book covers the articles on performance, utility and characteristics, and is the most important in the book.

"An Explanation for Speed" is probably Denhardt's best contribution to the Quarter Horse field. It is an attempt to describe the physical reasons for the unusual speed found in the Quarter Horse in short distances. The article entitled "Is the Quarter Horse a Thoroughbred?" is also one of the few good articles Denhardt has written. These articles can lay some claim to being fresh material, and not just a compilation or, more accurately, a rehash. These two articles explain the author's faith in the Quarter Horse and his firm belief that there is a place for this horse, not on the long track, but on the ranch, the rodeo, and the short track. Both of these have been widely reprinted.

"The Social Significance," by Dan and Jack Casement, gives the best outlook of the economic and social advance made possible by, with, and because of, the Quarter Horse. It demonstrates how the Quarter Horse has fit into the social-economic picture of the West. The reader will be a long time in forgetting the picturesqueness of this article. For example, while speaking of the Quarter Horse, "in his nick with the Texas Mustangs, their mutual product revealed the congenial characteristics of true soulmates," and, "Governmental subsidy of Thoroughbred breeding was all that was needed virtually to complete the job of weaning the affection of a lot of old-timers from their once cherished 'bulldogs,' who had stood by them in sickness and health, labor and levity, and to splice them to a fickle-headed, thinner-thighed, equine seductress." The last paragraph is equally good. You just cannot find writing any place that will compare with that which the Casements produce when they write together.

Albert Hand, writing for a California magazine, has written what is a most admirable tribute to the Quarter Horse. Apparently tired of having the Quarter Horse continually raked over the coals by uninformed breeders of other horses, he felt one who had always used, and who knew something first hand about them, should speak up for a change—and up he spoke. Every Quarter Horse man that reads this article, "Worth His Salt," has a warm place in his heart for Albert Hand, and knows that here writes a man who has lived with and on the greatest horse ever to look through a bridle.

Wayne Gard's story of Texas Quarter racing is probably the most interesting and best written of all the various stories on the subject. Gard, who is connected with the Dallas Morning News, is known as a writer. His best book is generally considered to be his work on Sam Bass.

PART ONE

Personal Observations and Reminiscences

Concho Colonel, His Life and Times

By DAN D. CASEMENT

THE HISTORY of the original horse that bore the name Steel Dust is clouded by the numerous legends concerning him. But Quarter Horses, of which race he is reputed to have been the most shining exponent, are with us today in every locality where cattle are handled in the open or where calf-roping or steer-wrestling contests are held, and there is scarcely a living range-man who cannot bear witness to their marvelous character, their smartness, their seemingly intuitive cow-sense, and their great speed at short distances.

Since, unfortunately, no official record or stud book has been established for the breed, our knowledge of its origin and history rests only on the stories handed down by old-timers of the western frontier and on the meager results of such research as has been made by a few of its most ardent admirers. As to the horse's wonderful qualities there is no lack of testimony. Every man who has ever ridden or owned one is usually extravagant in his praise, and every real Quarter Horse addict can recite endless stories of their prowess, always illuminated with picturesque names, romantic incidents, and thrilling accounts of dramatic victories in brush races.

Because all that is authentically known about this horse must be largely a compilation of personal recollection, it may not be out of place for me to make my contribution to the record by recounting here some incidents of my own experience.

Forty-five years ago, while running the "triangle bar" outfit in Western Colorado, I had the good fortune to own a typical Quarter gelding named Jackpaw. He worked cattle with the same instinctive zeal and efficiency that a field-trail dog hunts quail. When working him in a bunch, either cutting or roping, you seemed to share with him a sense of perfect unity and had a feeling of being atop a mighty mechanism like a coiled spring restrained by a delicate trigger. Reins or other aids were entirely superfluous. A rider's only concern was to indicate his desire, even in a most casual manner, and then to stay with him while Jackpaw executed it of his own accord.

The high regard for his race which Jackpaw inspired in me and the growing scarcity of such horses in our locality led to my determination to try to breed horses of this type. My own experience had influenced me in favor of small horses. At that time the men of the mountain ranges were demanding size in their mounts at the expense of handiness. I aspired to breed the type of horse which I personally liked, whenever I could find a promising mare and sire.

The type I accidentally discovered a number of years later portrayed in a copy of "Live Stock Markets," published then by Clay, Robinson & Co. There was pictured the Quarter Horse stallion, Brown Jug, that had recently been sold to the Correllitas Ranch in Chihuahua by William Anson, Christoval, Texas. Incidentally this ranch was later raided by Pancho Villa and Brown Jug was appropriated by him as his personal war-horse. Brown Jug was by Jim Ned. The horse I eventually bought was by the same sire. (See illustration facing page 135.)

Accompanying the picture was a short article by Mr. Anson from which I quote: "What is a Quarter Horse? Both the name and the breed are of remote origin in the United States. We find reference to them in the early chronicles of Virginia, called Quarter Horses, and answering the description they bear today. There seems little doubt that they were the original racing animals of the early planters of Virginia and the Carolinas. They subsequently found their way into Tennessee and Illinois, whence they were taken to Texas and the Southwest.

"The breed has always been kept in a comparative state of purity, the occasional mixture was often mutual, being attributed to some stallions which showed Quarter Horse characteristics either of shape or speed. We accordingly find that they have been bred absolutely true to type and that they have a wonderful power of transmitting their shape and qualities to their offspring.

"The immense breast and chest, enormous forearm, loin and thighs, and the heavy layers of muscle are not found in any other breed in the world in the same proportion. The desire for speed at short distances developed this type in distinction to that of the Thoroughbred, even as a hundred-yard champion is generally thickset and heavily muscled in comparison to the miler.

"As a breed they rarely exceed 15 hands, but attain great weight, many mature horses going as high as 1,200 pounds. In fact, you can find 'more horse to the height,' to speak colloquially, among Quarter Horses than in any other breed. This, in brief, is a description of a breed of horses unique in the world, a pure American breed, and one which is destined to play quite a part in the future of western ranches, a horse, be it noted, which does not dread the advent of the automobile."

On seeing the picture and reading the above statement, I wrote to Mr. Anson. A correspondence was thus begun which continued almost to the time of his death, although I met him only once during the years of our acquaintance. Notwithstanding his fondness for light horses, he was an importer and breeder of Suffolks and professed to see in that splendid British breed of punch-built farm drafters many of the characteristics which he admired so greatly in the Quarter Horse. Before I had met him and without previous inspection of either of the horses, I finally bought from him a stallion of each breed. Both proved to be super horses. Some of my most pleasant recollections, I am sure, will always be associated with Concho Colonel and Baby Charlee.

Billy Anson was a highly bred English gentleman and the younger son of a titled family distinguished in official circles of the Empire. He early sought his fortune as a rancher in West Texas and identified himself completely

BALLEYMOONEY
Balleymooney is the great Quarter Horse stallion purchased by Dan D. Casement from William Anson. Balleymooney was the sire who got such great sons and grandsons that today they are scattered all over the West, and are generally considered to be about the best stock of Quarter Horses available.

RED DOG
Red Dog is the present top stallion of the famous Casement Triangle Bar Ranch in the Unaweep Canyon, Colorado. He is owned by Jack Casement, and is a son of Balleymooney.

LITTLE STEVE
Little Steve was one of the great Quarter Horses of Colorado. He was by Pony Pete and out of Cherokee Maid. He is shown here when young and in running form.

DEXTER IN ACTION
Dexter was the best senior stallion at the Stamford Cowboy Reunion Quarter Horse show in 1941, and is owned by R. L. Underwood of Wichita Falls and was sired by Golden Chief.

with his unaccustomed surroundings. Although he never abated in the slightest degree the mannerisms in speech and behavior more usually encountered in fashionable London clubs than in Texas cow towns, he held, by virtue of his square shooting and upright qualities, the liking and respect of an exceedingly wide circle of friends among all classes of people. He was a thorough sportsman with a keen eye for a horse and very positive in his preferences, which he could defend ably and with sound reasons, backed by good plain horse-sense.

Apparently he had formed a high opinion of the Quarter Horse on sight and became at once an enthusiastic champion of the breed and the most intelligent and zealous student of the horse's history that has thus far appeared. At the time of the war in South Africa he held an important contract from the British government for the purchase of cavalry mounts and shipped thousands of horses out of Texas. In executing this contract he reserved a considerable number of the most typical Quarter mares that came into his hands and established a breeding establishment at his Head-of-the-River Ranch on the Concho.

In the course of our correspondence we soon discovered that our "horse notions" were completely congenial and I thus became a depository of a large fund of Quarter Horse lore, which he had accumulated by careful observation and research.

He insisted that the Quarter Horse was a distinct breed of American origin, developed by the colonists of Virginia and the Carolinas through selective breeding for the qualities that enabled these horses to excel in the sort of races most popular in those days. These events were mostly at short distances and were conducted under conditions which required contestants to be capable of the instant release of all their power, and to possess great intelligence coupled with a temperament immune to excitement under trying circumstances.

Such races are still run in the range country and only a good Quarter Horse can qualify successfully to meet the conditions. I have seen cowboys match races at 10 and 30 yards and then jockey an hour for a start on the "ask-and-answer" or "lap-and-tap" system. Such an ordeal calls for a level headed horse and since, when once started, the goal is reached in little more than a single jump, success depends on the horses' ability to break away with the swiftness and force of lightning. This accounts for the surprising muscular development characteristic of the Quarter Horse.

On the authority of such early writers on the American horse as Wallace and Herbert and on Edgar's Stud Book, Anson based his belief that the Quarter Horse was well established as a distinct breed in the Southern colonies prior to the time when the English Thoroughbred could have had much influence on colonial horse breeding. These writers clearly authenticate the existence in very early colonial days of the breed of horses called "Quarter-of-a-Mile Running Horses," the forbearers of the modern Quarter Horse.

"The only imported horse," wrote Anson, "which seems

to have had much influence on the breed was a horse called Janus." He adds somewhat facetiously, "From all accounts and the number of Januses which appear in old pedigrees, he must have been nearly as prolific as our own Texas Steel Dust, undoubtedly the most prolific horse that ever stood on four legs." Janus, he declared, is not in the English Stud Book and his pedigree has never been authenticated.

"I have heard," he wrote, "a dozen accounts of Old Steel Dust from men who knew him, all different, except in one particular. There is little doubt that he came from Southern Illinois, the home of so many 'short-horses.'"

Among the dozen Steel Dust stories, "all different," which Billy Anson had heard, the one which I am about to relate may have been included. It bears every mark of authenticity. To brand it as apocryphal would be to insult my kind informant, and yet I can believe it possible that some of the stories to which Billy gave a doubtful ear were similarly rich in plausible details.

Fifteen years ago I received a letter from William Williams, Denton, Texas, from which I quote: "I am less than 50 years old but my father is 89. He is well and hearty, was a ranger on the frontier, and is well up on all Texas history of the past. Many a time have I listened to stories of Steel Dust. Being a born horseman, I always liked stories about horses. Steel Dust, my father says, was brought to McKinney, Texas, in 1849 by the Batchler family. He was called a four-mile horse. They brought him there to match against Monmouth, which belonged to the Stiff family. Steel Dust was a quiet, gentle horse, very intelligent, and when he was led into McKinney, some of the witty ones of the crowd asked how they could wake him up. But that was no trouble, as he proved when the time came.

"It was said of him that when he was led out for a race he looked the crowd over very closely, as if to see who was there that he knew. Steel Dust was probably a Thoroughbred, as a mile was easy and he won the memorable race against Monmouth in two out of the three mile heats. That, my father says, almost bankrupted Collin County, as most men bet in those days, and, of course, they bet on the home horse. Two of his direct descendants were Yellow Wolf and Rocky Mountain Tom, both good at two or four furlongs."

Billy Anson, I'm sure, would have resented the intimation that Steel Dust was a Thoroughbred and a distance horse, for it contradicts his own well-founded conception of Quarter Horse origin and nature. But he doubtless would have welcomed and given full credence to Mr. Williams' statement relative to his direct descendants, Yellow Wolf and Rocky Mountain Tom, who were "both good at two or four furlongs." I find myself repeating these names because they are good examples of the rugged fashion in nomenclature which seems naturally to fit the Quarter Horse. Naturally, too, they seem to savor of the salty speech and raw fancies of rugged men, fit companions of the courageous horses that bore to lasting fame such names as Red Buck, Wild Cat, Pony Pete, Pecos Johnny, Dan Tucker, Little Steve and many others.

Although old Steel Dust appears to have been the original ancestor of the Quarter Horse of Texas and the Southwest, the names of some of his most notable descendants were later applied to offshoots of the breed which they themselves founded. Thus in certain sections Quarter Horses are known as "Billys," and are supposed to trace to one of Steel Dust's famous sons, while "Cold Decks," "Printers," and many recognized strains in other localities likewise inherit their titles from the sires that founded their own distinct branches of the breed.

In the early spring of 1911, Billy Anson wired me from Fort Worth an offer to sell Concho Colonel, one of the several stallions he then had at the Southwestern Exposition, where they had narrowly escaped the disastrous fire which swept the show grounds that year. He described him minutely, proposed to deliver him in Colorado Springs, where I was then living, and set his price at $500.00.

A few days before, I had learned of a horse owned by Charley Walker near Kiowa, Colorado, which could be bought for half that price and which, according to his description, seemed to be well suited to my purpose. I was just starting for the Walker ranch when Billy's telegram was delivered. I replied at once, explaining the circumstances and stating that I expected to buy the local horse. However, on inspection, The Senator, for that was his name, somehow did not seem to fill my eye. He was a rather sizeable chestnut, slightly sprung in the knees, lacking somewhat in symmetry, so I thought, and giving the impression of having seen better days.

My decision not to buy him may have been a mistake. A more discerning horseman doubtless would have recognized his excellence as a sire in the marvelous uniformity and quality of the large band of sorrel yearlings, his most recent product, which fairly overran the ranch. But I returned home and wired Billy that evening to send me his horse.

It is interesting—if not humiliating—to recall that ten years later "Senators" enjoyed such popularity among polo players as has not, to my knowledge, been equalled by the get of any other horse in my time. There was a veritable craze for them extending from California to Long Island. Players eagerly bought The Senator's progeny, often without seeing them and irrespective of their maternal ancestry or individual promise. The horse lived to a surprising age, eventually came into the hands of a prominent Denver horseman, and died honored as the sire of a great race of fleet and courageous horses.

The Senator, according to Charley Walker, was by a Thoroughbred horse named Leadville. So far as I know, Leadville's greatest distinction was achieved by siring this one notable son. It seems reasonable to believe, therefore, that The Senator's remarkable qualities were in the main inherited from his dam, who, Walker says, was a Quarter mare bearing the suggestive and unflattering name, "Wooley."

On the arrival of Concho Colonel I had my first introduction to a typical Steel Dust Quarter stallion. He was a beautiful dappled chestnut, compactly built, smooth and well balanced in shape, with short back, deep barrel and long belly. Most noticeable was his immense muscular development which seemed to reach a climax amounting almost to a positive deformity in his bulging jaws. Had he been a human, I would have suspected a bad case of the mumps. I subsequently learned that this appearance is characteristic of the Steel Dust strain. Indeed, in some localities Quarter Horses are commonly known as "Big Jaws."

Evidently it is this feature to which Billy Anson refers as "some coarseness in the head, which will be bred out in a few years of selection." Personally I shall welcome no such effort, for the persistence of this peculiarity seems to substantiate the theory that the dominant traits of the breed were indelibly fixed in remote generations, which doubtless accounts for the amazing uniformity found today in the get of a good Steel Dust stallion from mares of dissimilar types. These massive jaws seem to serve as a fitting symbol of the tenacity and determination which mark the Steel Dust strain. They make strange contrast to the alert little ears that denote the keenness of the horse's sensibilities, and furnish a substantial background for a forehead and eyes that bespeak deep stores of equine wisdom.

During the next 16 years, at our ranch in the Unaweep Canyon, close to the Utah line, The Colonel, as he was colloquially known, cut and roped cattle, sprinted in brush races, and herded in season a band of mares varying in numbers from 2 to 22, until he died at the age of 23. It is the fortunate fate of some exceptional horses to attain to the dignity of honored institutions in their communities by sheer force of character. Many, I'm sure, will testify that The Colonel owned this distinction. He was a great-hearted horse, wise, kind, loyal and brave.

In his career on that range he begot upwards of 130 foals that grew to maturity. In two successive years his harem trooped up in May, followed by 20 of his frolicsome sons and daughters. These youngsters, as yearlings or two-year-olds, we used to bring back to my Kansas farm, break out and then distribute to the four points of the compass. My records show that 112 of them went to 53 different owners in 16 states. Very few finished their schooling in our hands. Although some always served our needs in working the cattle, most of them left us when comparatively green. An old memorandum reveals that the 112 just mentioned brought a total of $16,782.36.

That sum, however, represents the smaller share of the actual profit which I personally gained from The Colonel and his numerous progeny. The more important part accrued to me in quite intangible form. It derived from the many hard falls they gave me and a broken bone or two—for there were few of them that I did not ride in the days of their apprenticeship. But principally it proceeded from the pleasure incident to a close, sympathetic and understanding companionship with the smartest string of colts I ever handled, and from the invaluable lessons they taught me. In truth, there was much that I learned about horses—and humans—from them.

In physical conformation they were strikingly alike. In the fundamentals of their character, which traced to their sire, they were sound and admirable. The innumerable, different kinds of deviltry, which all of them at times displayed, I can logically attribute only to the divers temperaments of their motley dams. But none of them were really vicious. Rather they may be properly described as horses of strong, distinctive character and indomitable will, brimful of *joie de vivre*.

In the Colonel's "yeguada" were mares of all sorts from Thoroughbreds to mustangs. My trip to Charley Walker's ranch, on which occasion I had turned down The Senator, had not been entirely fruitless, since it led to the purchase of 11 mares from the Walker band. Several of these were in foal to The Senator at the time, so that seven of his get were subsequently dropped in the Unaweep. To detail their adventures would require another chapter of these reminiscences. A strange sequel to that story, too, would disclose that the lovely Freehand mare, Gilpy, my personal mount today, is a granddaughter of this old horse, which 26 years ago I disdained.

In the Walker purchase were four Thoroughbred mares. Three others were by Little Steve and two were from dams by him. Little Steve and his get had acquired great fame in the early days of polo at Colorado Springs. Two of his full sisters, Mountain Maid and Croton Oil, had starred in the string of Foxhall Keene. All three had been bred by "Old Man" Smalley of Sylvan Grove, Kansas, a well-known "short-horse" man of his generation. Little

Steve was a Printer Quarter Horse by Pony Pete out of Cherokee Maid. His record for a furlong was 9-2/5 seconds; for a quarter, 22¼. (See illustration facing page 7.)

Five typical Spanish mares, remnant of a band of wild horses, which a neighboring ranchman had formerly run in New Mexico, were the least attractive of the Colonel's "manada" in point of shape and disposition. Plain western mares of no particular breeding completed his quota of mares.

On the issue of this heterogeneous harem The Colonel stamped a uniformity of conformation, color and character I have never seen equalled by the get of any other horse.

No sooner had these colts attained to some measure of maturity than they began to give a good account of themselves in various spheres of equine activity. Fireball, of the 1914 crop, out of one of the Thoroughbred mares, was twice champion polo pony at Santa Barbara in the ownership of Lafayette Hughes of Denver. Rosky, foaled in 1915 by one of the mustang mares, had quite a career as a playing pony in France and later was hunted successfully by his owner, Frederick Prince of Boston. I have heard him proclaimed by some of his admirers as a veritable wonder horse, seemingly indestructible.

This quality should be attributed, I think, largely to the blood of his drab little Spanish mother, for none of The Colonel's get surpassed in personality or quite equalled in stamina the colts from his five shabby bronco mares. I do not consider this circumstance miraculous but hold it to be in complete harmony with historic facts and the fundamental laws of nature, as I have tried to point out in previous articles on western horses.

In a catalogue of The Colonel's colts of this earlier period there is scarcely a name that fails to recall some ineffaceable memory. Nearly all of these scaramouches had a highly developed sense of drama; none were immune to temperamental explosions. What a string of incidents, grave and gay, are awakened by mere mention of the names of Baby Doll, Ladymouse, Mittens, The Little Colonel, Sticktite, Johnny-on-the-Spot, Judy O'Grady, Denise, Solagne, Germain, Brushwood Boy, Flamingo, Larkalong, Diana, Daphne, Dulce—(the latter three full-sisters, granddaughters of Little Steve)—Alexis, Caterer, Jazbo, San Simon, Zig Zag, Leopard Sweat, and innumerable others!

When I returned from France at the end of the war, I found The Colonel's progeny so abundant as well nigh to starve out the Herefords. Desperate measures were then necessary, so I advertised a sale in Grand Junction. To my surprise the auction was not the dismal fizzle I had expected.

Evidently these sprightly yearlings and twos had such strong appeal for a horse-loving public as to submerge its better judgment and temporarily to overcome its fears of economic insecurity. As if under a hypnotic spell, Austin Corcoran, the cowboy poet, bought a whole string of budding little stud horses, although he needed them no more than a cat needs six tails. Other buyers were equally reckless.

The last lot in the sale was the sorry little Mexican mare who, four years before, had foaled Rosky, the horse that later gained international fame, as above related. She went with a colt at foot to a rancher from Kanah Creek for $15.00. Turned out on the range, as soon as her new owner had weaned the colt, she promptly made her way back to the Unaweep, rejoined The Colonel's "manada" and subsequently mothered two more of his offspring. The younger of these, Roskito, is now owned by Mrs. Samuel Russell of Middletown, Conn. The other imparted to my son at a very early age an invaluable store of horse-sense. He broke her unassisted and for some years he and his filly were inseparable. Now, at the age of 17, she leads our band of six light brood mares on Juniata Farm, and has raised by three Remount stallions eight outstanding colts, all of whom unmistakably evince the strength and virtue of her Spanish blood.

I later recovered—in trade for a bull—her older brother, the weaner which the Kanah Creek cowman had taken home from the auction. This horse, Starlight, later had the distinction of being owned and honored to the last by my dear friend, Samuel Russell, the best all-around horseman I have ever known.

For two years following the sale The Colonel herded a depleted band. But in the spring of 1923 a partnership deal with Ed Springer of the C. S. Ranch at Cimarron, N. M., gave us an interest in 15 Quarter mares by his celebrated Steel Dust horse, Little Joe. On these mares The Colonel wrought with his wonted efficiency until he died.

The joint product equalled in all respects his previous accomplishments. Many of the progeny of these C. S. mares abide with me in pleasant memories, notably Coleen, which won The Grass-Riders Grub Stake at Fort Riley, and The Clipper, medal pony of the 11th Cavalry Club at Monterey.

One further incident of great importance to me marked The Colonel's career. I would like to record it here. Among the Walker mares was a quaint, soggy little personality that I had promptly chosen to be the future mother of The Colonel's successor. She was 12 years old at the time of purchase, and, I surmise, had been bred by "Old Man" Smalley. Named Little Judge, she was by Little Steve out of Sal by Grey Joe. Could one ask for a more mellifluous Quarter Horse pedigree?

Soon after her arrival in the Unaweep she dropped a filly foal by The Senator. This filly, named Olivia, I sold as a three-year-old in Colorado Springs; I thought at the time I had never seen a horse that so completely filled my eye. Many years later she died on Sam Russell's farm in Connecticut, having produced for him several very valuable colts.

In 1914 Little Judge dropped the miniature stud horse whose advent I awaited. We named him "Balleymooney." He began his individual life at weaning time most inauspiciously. When front-footed for branding he collided with the side of the pen so violently as almost to destroy himself, and hobbled through his first winter a pathetic, rickety little object.

But in his yearling fall he was brought back to Juniata Farm, soon outgrew the effects of his mishap, and came out in the spring the smoothest, shiniest, smartest, most attractive thing one could imagine. For years "Bally" was the farm's most remarkable character. He had the quality of inspiring affection by his intelligence, his beauty and the charm of his personality. He was deeply understanding and delightfully companionable. I repress the temptation to recite some examples of his remarkable sagacity to avoid taxing the reader's credulity. Our appreciative assessor seemingly sought to reflect the community's esteem for "Bally" by persistently refusing to list him on the tax schedule. (See illustration facing page 6.)

After he had been with us at Juniata 16 years, I loaded him in a trailer and hauled him behind my Model A over the Rockies to his birthplace, a journey of nearly 900 miles. There he survived only one season, herding ten of his sire's relicts, the best of the C. S. mares. He died that winter, but, when spring came around, seven little "Ballys" and two filly foals made their advent, as if to dispel all doubt of his immortality.

Bally's spirit still animates the Unaweep Ranch in the presence there of three of these colts, entire and now four-year-olds, Red Dog, Frosty and Buck Shot. Another, The Deuce, a perfect replica of his sire, I have brought back to Juniata Farm, forsaking henceforth the use of all Remount Thoroughbreds so long as we both shall live. It is true that 13 youngsters by Stormy Port, the mighty Porter's son, work our cattle and graze our pastures at present, but The Deuce's first foals are now dropping and in three years we expect to be mounted once more on horses that know instinctively how to handle cows.

I must acknowledge that the modern craze among polo players for Thoroughbred size, weight and sustained speed has pushed the Quarter Horse into the background of the game. Steel Dust enthusiasts have observed this tendency with regret and some resentment. Against their better judgment it has turned some horsemen aside from their early attachment. Even so staunch a devotee of the Quarter Horse as Bill Anson suffered qualms of indecision, as he confessed in one of his last letters to me. But I shall let no such consideration lessen my loyalty and devotion to a breed which above all others has supplied in fullest measure for nearly a half century the qualities I love best in a horse.

He Was Called Billy

By H. T. FLETCHER

NO STRAIN OF HORSE has more of the romantic in its history than the Quarter or Billy Horse. It is the romance of the race, the carnival, the rodeo and the cowcamp. It is the glamour of hard rides and narrow escapes from outlaws and by outlaws. For, apart from the popularity of Quarter Horses on the race courses at fairs and carnivals, every desperado had a penchant for either raising or stealing good, fast horses. John Wesley Hardin, a famous Texas outlaw, wrote in his memoirs, while in prison, of his Quarter stallion Frank, through whose speed he escaped more than one posse and noose.

We have been interested in raising good cow horses for nearly twenty years, and, having used several Quarter stallions in the breeding of our present stock mares, Quarter blood predominates. Apart from my personal experience and observation, I have accumulated, around camp fires and from old-timers, a varied assortment of Quarter Horse facts and lore. Having been keenly interested in the articles by Dan D. Casement and others, I desire to contribute my bit, with the hope that some reader may find it of interest.

Just after the Civil War, William Fleming brought a colt from Kentucky to Belmont, Gonzales County, Texas. This was at that time the heart of the leading stock-raising section of the state. This colt was said to be descended from Steel Dust, the latter supposedly a registered Thoroughbred. He was called Billy, and, according to all accepted Thoroughbred standards, was a "sport." That he was a true "sport" is shown by his establishing a new type and the uniformity with which his increase have perpetuated that type.

Billy was described to me by a neighbor who saw him many times on his home farm and knew his owner well. He was a brown-bay, 14¾ hands tall, and weighed around 1,000 pounds. His body was heavy, his hips were sloping, and legs comparatively short. His neck was short and smoothly joined to his trunk; he carried his trim head low. Pretty, tapering ankles and small feet complete the

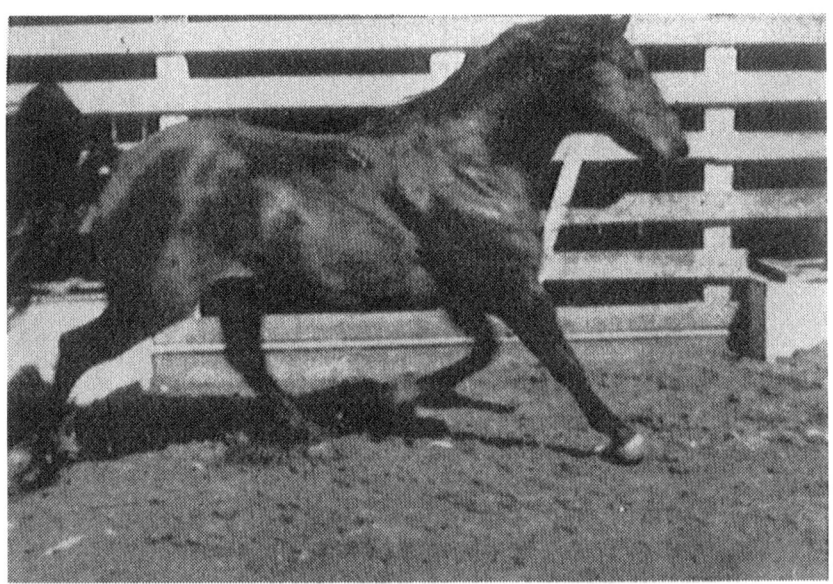

LOBO IN ACTION
Lobo was one of the best Billy Quarter stallions in the United States until his death a few years ago. He was owned by J. F. Hutchins of Pierce, Texas. He was sired by Spokane, the great sire of Raymond Dickson. Few know and love Quarter Horses like these two Texans.

BILLY BYRNE
This Arizona stallion, owned by J. E. Browning of Willcox, is one of the outstanding Casement bred stallions in the West. He was sired by Balleymooney.

GEORGE CLEGG

The dun stallion that is owned by Benny Binion of Dallas, Texas, and was raised by Bert Benear of Tulsa, Oklahoma, from stock originally purchased from George Clegg of Alice, Texas.

TOM BENEAR

Tom Benear is a great grandson of Yellow Wolf and Hickory Bill, and was bred by Bert Benear of Tulsa, Oklahoma. He is owned by Guy Troutman of Tucumcari, New Mexico.

description of our first Quarter Horse; for, strange to say, the changed conformation had reduced his running distance to a quarter of a mile.

To this good day no county fair, carnival or Fourth of July celebration is complete without its quarter of a mile race, and every community in South and West Texas has a Billy Horse that it will back with its money. The Billy strain became popular in South Texas, and Billy's sons and grandsons carried on in hundreds of studs. From this fountain-head the strain spread over Texas and even into other states. Mr. Fleming bred Billy Horses for more than forty years. In 1875 he and John King, a neighbor, started a Billy stud book. I have made numerous inquiries, but as the principals have been dead many years I can learn nothing of its whereabouts.

Among Billy's famous sons were Red Rover, Jim Brown and Midnight. Joe Murray, a grandson, was brought to Brewster County by L. F. Buttrill in 1887. Other stallions were brought in, and the Big Bend became and is today a Billy stronghold. The Billy was a great improver of the Spanish stock of horses, and this mixture tended to overcome the only fault of the Billys—soft bones and light pastern joints. These are not noticeable faults on soft ranges or race courses, but quite serious in a rough, rocky country. As colts, Billy Horses are often difficult to gentle, "pitching" long and hard, but they seem to possess a poise and calmness which, with their courage and quickness, makes an admirable combination for cutting horses.

Many years ago George McGonigle, father of Clay,

celebrated as champion steer roper of the world, moved from South Texas to Midland County, on the South Plains, and carried with him a stock of Billy Horses. For this stud many new stocks were no doubt recruited. In later years Rowdy, half-Billy from the McGonigle stock, won everlasting fame as the rodeo horse upon which Clay McGonigle made the all-time world championship record of 19 seconds for roping and tying a steer. Rowdy was longer-bodied than the typical Billy, and was almost human in his manner of taking advantage of a steer. He belonged to "Joe" Gardner, a friend of Clay, who on him previously made the fast time of 21 seconds at San Antonio. A strange coincidence is that Clay McGonigle died last fall [1921] in Arizona, and "Joe" Gardner died within a short time at Sierra Blanca, Texas. These two had roped thousands of times on old Rowdy and toured much of the world together. I saw Clay at Phoenix in 1919, at the State Fair, riding a fine horse and herding for the "bronc" riders.

Just a word as to the breeding of Steel Dust, to which Billy is supposed to trace. "Steel Dust" is a term used today, in the Southwest at least, to denote horses supposed to trace to the stallion Steel Dust. I have a letter before me in which the registrar of the American Studbook says: "While we have heard of the term 'Steel Dust' used in connection with the Texas ponies to which you refer, we have no idea as to their real origin. A number of years ago applications frequently were received from breeders in Texas to register with us animals that were not strictly

Thoroughbred and were known as 'appendix' animals, their ancestors tracing to animals registered in the appendix to the American Studbook, the publication of which appendix has been discontinued. It may be that the Steel Dust pony is a descendant of one of these families."

Among race horses tracing to Billy may be mentioned Ace of Hearts, Little Joe, and Arch Oldham. Ace of Hearts, at thirteen years of age, was unhitched from a wagon, and ran his first race and afterward won races all over South and West Texas. He was raced at Marathon in this county. Little Joe, in his prime, was said to be the fastest horse alive in Texas. Arch Oldham was the fastest half-mile horse ever raised in Texas, and was brought to Brewster County some eight years ago. Last year he was still doing service at eighteen years of age.

Six years ago W. P. Fischer, Marfa, Texas, bought from William Anson a five-year-old stallion which he called Crawford Sykes. Last spring we acquired him by exchange, and his colts are dropping right along now. Mr. Fischer has some fine colts just ready to break, and a few good ones already gentle. He is a brownish-bay and the description given of old Billy will nearly fit him. He has a wonderful disposition. Mr. Anson used him several years at his Christoval ranch. I wrote to Crawford Sykes, Pandora, Texas, for information regarding him. I quote from his reply:

"I raised the horse you speak of, and sold him to Billy Anson as a two-year-old for $150.00. His sire was Arch Oldham. I gave $1,000.00 for Arch. His sire was Gallantry.

Arch was a race horse from the word go to ⅝ of a mile. His dam I do not know. The mother of your horse was sired by Rondo, the best horse to sire Quarter Horses—I mean ¼-mile race horses—that ever was between the San Antonio and Guadalupe Rivers. The first I ever knew about Billy Horses was about 45 years ago, owned by Bill Fleming on the Guadalupe, near Belmont. As for a record book, I cannot say. Fleming is dead years ago and his stock of horses gone. The old original Billy was the sire of McCoy Billy, and McCoy Billy the sire of Rondo. Rondo sired your horse's mother. The best Quarter Horses are all gone from here."

Mr. Sykes is nearly 80 years of age, and bred Billy Horses nearly 50 years. It is a pity the Quarter Horse cannot have a competent historian while many of the old breeders are still alive. They fill an important economic need and their number should never be allowed to grow less.

Master of Two Trades

By JACK S. CASEMENT

WHEN ASKED why we breed Quarter Horses, we generally revert to age-old "short-horseman" custom—we forget all about cattle and other everyday interests, and find our tongue hinged in the middle, giving reasons limited only by printable vocabulary.

The true start to a disciplined reply to that question,

however, doubtless should be the frank confession that being raised on (and off) them may very likely have had something to do with it. More than 28 years ago this outfit, already 28 years in the cattle and horse business, started to pull in its open range operations. Part of that retrenchment program was the founding of both a registered Hereford herd, and a pure as possible Steel Dust Quarter Horse stud, both run year-round on the meadows.

That was long enough ago to make this writer's almost first mounts, first colts to break, and first track-hopefuls all descendants of the Little Steve "Printer" strain, and the Jim Ned line of Billy Anson. Their blood was, in the early '20's, refortified by Peter McCue infusions—that is, via fillies descended from Anson's Harmon Baker. Replacement of this second band of old sisters was not necessary until my third generation of proprietorship, until a suitable third generation stud had been bred, track tried, and also found endowed with cow sense. Improvements on those mares were hard to locate in this age of subsidized Thoroughbred breeding, but granddaughters of Peter McCue's and Old Fred's were finally found.

To claim freedom from plain kid prejudice would be farcical in view of those so fortunate early environmental facts. But several seasons' work for wages with one-half to seven-eighths Thoroughbreds, plus more seasons mounted on almost everything the Southwest could offer in the way of supposed Morgans, obviously part Standard Breds, half breeds, and just plain Indian-Spanish blood refined and ornery-fied by that of the Percheron Puddin' Foot should, it would seem, have sufficiently tempered that prejudice to make it as tolerable as that of the next professional tout. Early environment and propinquity, then, kindled the flame of this Quarter Horse affection. It was early rationalized, likewise, upon fairly honest horse-sense premises. The most outstanding equine attribute in its relation to man is the speed its cultivation gives him, which, in turn, makes him master over all other domestic and semi-wild animals. Speed alone can be attained by man with machinery, but speed usable in the pastoral pursuits can still only be gained by mounting oneself on hot equine blood. The issue, fortunately, between the various warm blooded breeds is not at all clouded. It is impossible for any other breed to fully extend the Quarter Horse for distances less than that for which he has for several hundred years been bred, conditioned, and named. And, since the Quarter Horse has largely been bred on the range with cattle, has generally received his breaking, and usually earned his oats between races at cow work, he is the naturally evolved master of two trades.

Centuries of specialization enhance him today with an inner and outer beauty mighty pleasing to the pragmatic senses of anyone engaged in stock raising; every contour of his conformation is a reflection of the muscle-mechanics which make him the master of all other breeds in pure feet-per-second; every hidden nerve and reflex has so long been conditioned to stock work that now it is merely a matter of stimulating a green Quarter colt by the presence of stock in order to have him automatically respond on account of the similarity between their basic principles of conformation. Just as one seeks for and, to an extent, finds really great thickness, depth of body, and meat on quarters and shoulders, carried far down toward hock and knee, all on the shortest possible wheelbase, in our modern Herefords, so one finds exactly the same thing in a true Quarter Horse, only in place of edible meat we have the muscle of matchless speed.

The packers claim they can't get too much beef in too small a package. They cry for a minimum of head, neck, and lower legs; a maximum of body weight for the least length and height. A "short horse" man, likewise, seeks to send his colors out on the back of something small headed, short necked, with knees and hocks close to the ground, with forearms and stifles real component parts of great shoulders and quarters. They find that a widespread fork is just as sure an index of speed as a short coupling. A back which is all loin is their goal. They know that the most horse per hand-of-height is the winner in any dash. And most cowmen agree that these characteristics make the Quarter Horse the stoutest on the end of a rope, the handiest to cut on in a herd, and both safest and fastest when heading off a wild one hightailing it down hill over down timber.

Doubtless the minds of all animals (including man) are to their bodies much as one side of a stamped medallion is the obverse of the other. Certainly the Quarter Horse is psychologically adapted to the trade to which he is so well physically fitted just as much as is the smart, small, but sinewy kid who jockeys him, or the seemingly split-out-of-oak range hand who endures with him the grilling, endless, annual cycles of cow work, yet whose psychic reactions in cutting cattle, even after 40 years in the saddle, are slower than those of a knowing horse used in the bunch only a few seasons. Give a "short-horse" man a good colt of true Quarter Horse conformation, and with very little schooling he will show you horse intelligence and disposition ideally adapted to breaking off dash starts (at which all feet must be flat on the ground), where the most unphlegmatic hot bloods simply become nervous wrecks. He will show you a mind that will compel its body to give absolutely everything in even the shortest race. Likewise, if he is also a stockman, he will show you horse perspicacity sufficient to head off a cow's move before she has made up her mind to make it. Yet this is just the natural obverse of a physique capable of spotting a cow ten yards and still catching her seemingly before she starts.

In other words, one who depends upon bulls and studs for his bread and butter has a right to choose and peddle the Quarter variety of the latter for really a host of closely related reasons. Not the least of these is that the Quarter stud is as pleasurable a companion as would be some old top hand risen from the bygone trail herd days, to say nothing of being just as useful and educational to have around. Geldings probably do the showier job of hackamore work, rope work, and exhibition weaner-yearling cutting. A Quarter stud really wide between the eyes and mature in range mare herding and stock work is far too smart to put on an exhaustingly flashy rein demonstration. Take your rope down on one, and he is generally too anxious to eat his calf up, bust wide open, and finish his part of the job pronto, to give his rider a smooth lay or easy stop. Take him in the bunch, and an old stud never works his ears as enchantingly as do his emasculated sons. He lays them back so tightly that they become invisible, and bares his teeth. Then he builds to the designated critter with a show of anger, and an apparent sense of vengeance at having to get an unpleasant task over with in order to get back to resting again, like that which he exhibits when after a recalcitrant mare whose wanderings have disturbed his regal pasture peace. Needless to say, he gets his work done with calculated dispatch if not daintiness. It takes no mind reader to see that most studs study not only during their pasture seasons, but even while they are drowsing around the corral between saddles.

W. D. Wear's Frosty, in his adolescence here, used to work out a pasture of registered heifers (with whom he endured celibacy) one by one around the neck of a swamp which divided the meadow almost in two. When confined to the limits of our miscellaneous lot, that the cattle might not sacrifice too much tallow in the acquisition of sound wind, he worked to death both a milk cow and a pet goat. He also always used to test out his rider at regular intervals, just to be sure that he was sufficiently awake to take care of himself in case a critter suddenly needed heading. Such behavior, however, was an exuberance of youth which disappeared about the time his jaws got their full bulge. (See illustration facing page 198.)

His brother, Red Dog, who has been more or less in charge here for several years, was a totally different colt personality. His one idea was to get all work over with as soon as possible. To this end he studied ways and means at his leisure, but deemed practice at pasture a waste of valuable energy which he might some day badly need in a pinch. He early discovered that, if he could throw a sufficient boo into a sultry heifer by a burst of literally biting speed in the first few rods before she het up, he could trail, point, and pen her any place, from such a leisurely distance that both of them kept cool. He still looks upon all men with obvious contempt. He can spy mares far further than can his rider, and always salutes them so deafeningly that they quit the country in fear and trembling—the only place at all where he fails to let his head save his feet. (See illustration facing page 6.)

Balleymooney, his sire, was just as much a student of the philosophy of looking after Number One. And Concho Colonel, the grandsire, who came here from Texas 28 years ago, was probably as rugged an individualist as was ever on a ranch.

Arabian mares, they say, are not only the dominant sex of the breed back in their own country, but are practically human tent companions. Stallions, to our way of thinking, certainly seem to have more than their purely chance sex's rightful share of Quarter Horse personality and character; yet the mares make real hands, and we break and work all replacement fillies rather than ride geldings.

No more need be told of those Steel Dust stud instincts for self-preservation, both so vast yet so basically human, that we necessarily hedonistic individuals, whose only social security resides in our own resources, unconsciously profit by their cultivation. So is it any wonder we have stuck to the same satisfactory stud line through three generations, preferring to renew blood ever so often by going out and collecting totally different mare bands? Or to what other breed could we logically pledge our affection on a firmer foundation?

Cold Deck and Short Races
By GENE M. MOSES

THE MINING CAMPS of Southwest Missouri were once the center of Quarter Horse racing. It may be of interest to horsemen to hear of the races and trace the origination of some of the greatest Quarter Horses of the past.

According to "old-timers" who owned, trained and raced the fastest horses of the late 80's and early 90's, Cold Deck was the greatest sire of Quarter Horses in this country. Cold Deck was brought out of Tennessee a few years after the Civil War and was raced at short distances for several years. "Uncle" Tom Stogdon, who is now past 80 years old and lives northeast of Alba, Missouri, knew Cold Deck well and owned him several different times.

"Uncle" Tom described Cold Deck as being a heavy built chestnut, weighing about 975 pounds and slightly under 15 hands. He was heavily muscled, was exceptionally well ribbed, and had a very "breedy" head. His legs were short from hock to ankle and from knee to ankle. He had considerable Thoroughbred blood but no one knows how much. Some people say he had an ugly disposition, but "Uncle" Tom contradicts the statement and says that he was high strung, but level-headed when on the mark for a race.

There are few descendants of the original Cold Deck, except through two of his colts, Big and Little Mike. The Mikes, as the family is commonly called by Quarter Horse men, have produced many fast "short horses," but none as good as those from mares sired by Cold Deck. One of the Mike horses stood at Lamar, Missouri, for many years and his colts were much in demand for racing purposes. There is a grandson of this horse at that town now, but he appears more like a common plow horse than a race horse.

The writer has made several trips into northeast Oklahoma for the purpose of locating some of the direct descendants of Cold Deck through the mare line and has only found one horse that can be traced direct to the original on reliable information.

This horse is of good conformation for a short distance race horse or for polo. His sire is a registered Thoroughbred and his dam is a true Cold Deck. He is as much like Cold Deck in build, color and disposition as two horses could be, according to men who have seen both animals. He has run a large number of matched races at from three hundred yards to three-eighths of a mile, but was most successful at a quarter of a mile.

In the days when Quarter Horse racing was popular in this district, it was a common sight to see a covered wagon come into the small towns with two or more ponies tied behind. Shortly after camp was made, usually near the straight course where the races were run, a crowd would gather and the conversation between the newcomer and one of the local Quarter Horse men would be about as follows:

"Howdy, pardner. Where you-all pull in from?"

"I come up from Fort Smith."

"That bay mare you-all got there looks as though she might run a little."

"Yeah, she is a right nice mare, but I got two more that can make her hump. Don't know anyone that would like to match up a race, do you?"

"Well, I don't know but what I might have something for you to try and beat for fifty or a hundred."

"Here's a hundred to put up. Get yours down and bring your horse around Sunday morning."

"How far do you want to make it?"

"Call it yourself. Just draw a line and walk down the road until you get tired and put down a stake. That will be where we start and finish. My horse will be there first or you got a hundred to spend."

From then on the onlookers would start making up bets among themselves and telling about all the races they could remember and many they had never seen or heard about.

By the time to race perhaps the newcomer would get

down many more bets, consisting of harness, wagon, jack-knife, rifle, and last, but most important, his coon dog.

Little boys were usually carried along for jockeys. A saddle pad or wadded blanket held on by a surcingle served for a saddle and oftentimes they rode bareback.

Bull of the Woods, Gray Jane, Joplin Belle, Madam Bishop, Bad Eye, Pay Dirt, and, of course, Cold Deck, were fast Quarter Horses with wide reputations in the district covered by northeast Oklahoma, southeast Kansas, northwest Oklahoma and southwest Missouri.

It was common for a man to win several thousand dollars with a good pony in the Indian Territory. Most of the Indians were easily talked into a race and generally lost all they bet as their ponies were inferior to the good Quarter Horses taken through their country.

Races are run over straight courses for short distances in many parts of Oklahoma now. In the mining towns of Picher, Commerce and Miami several matched races are run each week. All conceivable schemes are employed to win money from the spectators who gather to see the ponies run. A common stunt these days is for a party to camp out on the prairie and wait for a motorist to drive along the road in a high-powered car. He is stopped and engaged in conversation leading up to a challenge to race a horse against the automobile. The driver is usually a mining man or oil man who has considerable means and of the type who welcomes a challenge. The horse and the car go from a standing start, and as the distance is usually not over 300 yards, the horse wins easily. One pony called

Teddy R. is said to have beaten every kind of high-priced car on the market. The writer owned this pony for a short time, and often wondered, when riding, why he would jump when a car went past him. Later I learned of his past history.

An ordinary good Thoroughbred in training could win from the average Quarter Horse run in this country as very few run faster than 24 seconds for a quarter of a mile. However, the racing ponies get very little preparation for a race and can run remarkably fast considering the conditions under which they are handled, and it must be remembered they are not scored.

It appears as though they are considered a breed to themselves by some people as it is not uncommon to hear owners discussing strains and families. Of course, some of the ponies are simply crosses of Thoroughbreds and common bronc mares, but there are several of the best that have no crosses of Thoroughbred blood for several generations.

The general run of racing ponies is of good conformation, flat bone, exceptionally heavy quarters, and of quiet disposition until excited or mistreated. They are game and willing little horses that are easily kept, and can stand lots of hard knocks. If properly trained, they should prove valuable as polo mounts.

The statement that they naturally have quiet dispositions may not seem to follow with speed and "fast breaking." But the truth of this statement is borne out by the fact that rodeo performers have purchased these ponies of late years and used them for "roping" and "bulldogging." The speed of their mounts in catching a steer is in no small measure responsible for their success in winning contest prizes. One well-known performer uses a pony that was raced at Picher, Oklahoma, several years. He had no difficulty in training him to run down steers without guiding and to stop when the steer was caught.

For pleasure riding purposes pure Quarter Horses have little to recommend them. They do not have much style compared to saddlebred animals and usually move at a slow walk. Their trot is short and stubby, generally speaking, but most of them do have a slow, easy canter that is a pleasure to ride. Even after several years of racing, they cannot be brought to traveling with other horses without trying to run every time pressure on the bit is reduced. If challenged by another horse, however, all that is necessary to get them away at top speed is a lurch forward in the saddle, or perhaps a slight kick in the ribs with the heels.

The writer is an admirer of pure Thoroughbreds and does not consider Quarter-bred stock as race horses in comparison.

I Do Not Like Him
By GROVE CULLUM

DO RIGHT and fear no man. Don't write and avoid embarrassing questions. I wrote a series of articles in which I discussed the Quarter Horse, his probable origin and his present-day usefulness. Now, the chickens are coming home to roost. The last month has brought many inquiries and comments on statements I have made.

DEL RIO JOE

Del Rio Joe was the purple ribbon Quarter Horse at the first official American Quarter Horse Association Show, held at Stamford, Texas, in 1940. He was raised by L. B. Wardlaw of Del Rio, Texas. He is a grandson of Harmon Baker on both his dam and sire's side. His sire's dam was a grandson of Jim Ned, and his dam's dam was sired by Little Joe. Note the great resemblance between Del Rio Joe and his double grand sire, Harmon Baker. (See illustration of Harmon Baker facing page 86.)

LUCKY STRIKE

Lucky Strike is the beautiful Quarter Horse stallion owned by Will Northington of Egypt, Texas. He was sired by the Old Sorrel and out of Panchita, and bred on the King Ranch.

SQUAW

Squaw was a daughter of Old Fred, and out of a Peter McCue mare. She was one of the fastest horses of her day, winning 49 out of 50 starts. She was bred by Coke Roberds of Hayden, Colo.

Some ask for elucidation, others charge me with prejudice against the Quarter Horse.

Let's get the record straight. I have no prejudices against the Quarter Horse. I simply do not like him for any purpose I know of—with one possible exception. I am told by those who have had experience that in rodeos he is excellent. This, I can understand. He has a quick getaway, plenty of speed for short dashes, a heavily muscled body on short legs—all to his advantage. Due to the type of saddle used, his defective shoulders and withers present apparently no insurmountable handicap.

I have never roped a steer and never hope to rope one, but if I should, my horse would have good shoulders and good withers. Otherwise, I would not be on him. Again, this is not prejudice, it is the fruit of experience. Many of the best roping horses and some of the best polo ponies carry a very considerable strain of Quarter Horse in their inheritance. But they possessed good shoulders and good withers which they got, in all probability, from some Thoroughbred ancestor.

It is true that a Quarter Horse has powerful loins and a powerful croup. But a good horse has more than one good end—he has two good ends, a good middle-piece, and good underpinning.

The question of breeding should be approached with an open mind and a clear conception of one's purpose. What market does one wish to reach? For what purpose is the produce to be used? Or is one breeding purely as a hobby, caring not a whit for the opinions of others or the demands of a market? And even if the last is the object, the breeder must practice some selection and elimination, unless he is just breeding at random, in which case all he has to do is close his knife, open his gates, and come spring the horses will breed by themselves.

But let's assume the object is to breed good polo prospects, or hunters, or hacks, or just useful riding horses. In this case, would I use either a stud or mares of the typical Quarter Horse family? I would not. I have already admitted that some of the best are produced by a Quarter Horse-Thoroughbred cross. But the percentages are all against the breeder. For each good one so produced there are far too many misfits. And why is this true?

To begin with, the Quarter Horse is one of the oldest breeds in America, antedating by many generations the introduction of the Thoroughbred. He existed in the early Colonial days, and possessed then the same characteristics that he has today. This alone tends to explain his remarkable prepotency today—that is, his ability to stamp his get with his own characteristics. Unfortunately, he has only two attributes worth perpetuating — a heavily-muscled body and short legs.

The virtue of even these must be questioned. While his muscles are heavy, they are short and too frequently not well attached to a framework that is poorly cast for a horse expected to give a smooth, well-balanced ride—one that is expected to stop and turn quickly and smoothly from top speed, one that must stay when temperatures are high, humidity is great, going is soft. And this is not theory; it is fact. Let the skeptical inquire of someone who has played a typical Quarter Horse on Long Island in July.

His legs have the one virtue of being short, but his joints are shallow and round, and his tendons are poorly placed. Too often he is boggy in the hocks, cocked in the ankles, and back at the knees. And, isn't there such a thing as a body too heavy on legs that are too short? A hippopotamus is a heavily bodied animal on very short legs, but so far as I know no one ever tried to ride a hippopotamus.

So my reason for saying I would not breed to either a stud or mares that are typical of the Quarter Horse family are: (1) He is remarkably prepotent and (2) he has, and always has had, too many faults simply ruinous to a good riding horse.

True, an infusion of Quarter Horse blood has been known to help the Thoroughbred for general purposes by contributing a more massive musculature. But this result divorced from attendant faults is so rare that to breed for it seems hopeless. Unfortunately, the laws of heredity permit us no choice between the characters and attributes of sires and dams that are to be reproduced and those to be eliminated.

A very young man once told me his plans for breeding the super cowhorse. From a touch of Arab he was to get intelligence; from the Thoroughbred, speed and shape; from the Morgan, hardiness; from the Quarter Horse, muscle; and from the old Spanish horse a sort of sixth sense, called cow-sense. All this was to be accomplished by observing the phases of the moon and the signs of the zodiac. . . . Well, superstition is a difficult ghost to slay. Cut in two, like the horsehair snake, one end grows a new head, the other a new tail, and we have two snakes instead of one.

Breeding at best is a gamble. Were it not so, individuality would gradually disappear and horses would be turned out in models. Indeed, under a Fascist regime the same might happen to the human family. But since the Creator was, I imagine, neither a Fascist nor a Nazi, we may trust ova and spermatozoa to continue the production of individuals no two of which shall be exactly alike.

The most that the breeder can do is to reduce to a minimum his chances of variation from his selected ideal. And how is this to be done? To begin with, real success is rarely, if ever, achieved without a certain amount of intelligent effort and painstaking care.

For example, last year I received from a friend a letter which states in effect: "I decided to breed horses . . . I saw a Steel Dust stallion . . . was so impressed with his extraordinarily heavy muscles that I bought him . . . I have been breeding him for a year or so and now I should like to know something about him."

Personally, *before* purchasing him I should have wanted to know a lot about him and his ancestry. I would have known, first of all, my goal; the market I hoped to reach or the type I wanted to produce. Once decided, I would select the stallion and mares that have individually as many as possible of the desired traits and characters. Moreover, I should want them to come from families that possessed these same attributes in marked degree. Then, as soon as a fair judgment of results could be made, I should start ruthlessly to eliminate dams and possibly the sire.

There is nothing new in this theory. It comes from Johann Gregor Mendel, who conducted his fascinating experiment with peas to discover the principles of dominant and recessive characters, as well as other principles explaining the laws of heredity. The value of his discoveries have been proved over and over again by laboratory experiments as well as by practical breeders.

The Quarter Horse was once the apple of my eye. That, however, was before I tried him, before I learned that his tribe could give the most uncomfortable down-hill ride, blow up quicker, and fall down harder than any horse I had ever owned or ridden before or since. Perhaps I am too rough on the Quarter Horse, but I do insist that these are opinions based on experience, not on prejudice; I have neither Quarter Horses nor Thoroughbreds to sell.

It is easy to appreciate the dilemma that confronts the average breeder, especially in the West. Say "Thoroughbred" to him, and he pictures a leggy, fine-boned, bowed-tendoned, wasp-waisted frantic creature being hauled and mauled into a starting shoot, only to dart out again. And you cannot blame him. Out in our western country he has seen too many of these. He hasn't seen many of those big-boned, deep-bodied, level-headed, strong, useful-looking Thoroughbreds that have the power of a Joe Louis, the speed of a Glenn Cunningham, the intelligence of an Einstein, the tenacity of John Bull himself.

Naturally, the Quarter Horse, with his heavily muscled body on short legs and his apparently even disposition, makes a strong appeal to the western breeder. Especially is this true if, as is generally the case, he is not a discriminating judge of the less obvious but nonetheless important details such as length and slope of shoulder, height and strength of wither, placing of tendons, and many other details.

Also, the use of a Thoroughbred sire does not insure success. But it may be said that if one is breeding horses for use under the saddle, his only hope of gaining outstanding success in the general market lies in the use of a Thoroughbred sire with mares that carry a preponderance of Thoroughbred qualities. A large percentage of the offspring so bred should, if properly nurtured, develop into useful and saleable horses. A few of them are almost certain to be outstanding.

It has been said, "Build a better mousetrap and the world will beat a path to your door." Of this I am skeptical, but I do believe that "Produce a superior horse and horse buyers will wear out the path to your door."

I Object

By JACK S. CASEMENT

"DON'T WRITE and avoid embarrassing questions," began Major Grove Cullum, former chief of Remount, speaking from his wide experience about the Quarter Horse. Such an article, I feel sure, is an embarrassing question only to his friends.

To men devoting their lives to general horse improvement through commercial distribution of the various Quarter Horse strains in direct and unsubsidized competition with the Remount Service, his statement sounds like a malicious insult, since it comes from one who, obviously with facts to the contrary in his possession, deliberately falsifies them to propagandize a pet prejudice.

Would anyone think of denying prejudice so repeatedly had he a clear conscience? Could anyone not prejudiced write an article, a fair and just synopsis of which is, in his own words, "I simply do not like the Quarter Horse for any purpose I know of"—in the face of his unbeatable track records?

"The Quarter Horse was once the apple of my eye," Cullum admits. The particular "apple" with which he illustrated a chapter on Quarter Horses in his book on various breeds happens to have been a stud bred by my father, the sire of the stallions both my father and I and several others are using exclusively and profitably today.

Coupled with this is the fact that for the last two years two of the winners of the great Tucson stock horse show for working cowhorses have been by this same stud and carry my brand. (Proof that Cullum knew Quarter Horse value once!) And these studs were put up in that show over Thoroughbreds by men whose lifelong experience with light horses, in the laboratory of the range where now alone light horses are still in contact with the realities of life, gives a weight to their pronouncements not found in those of huntsmen and polo players, to whom horses are primarily things of pleasure.

Together, perhaps, these circumstances excuse my presumption in seeking to prove the former Remount chief has put out something mighty close to slander.

First let me submit what is believed to be a better founded statement of Quarter Horse origin than that found in his footnote. Quarter-mile racing was *the* sport in Virginia in 1690, and Virginia horses were all descended, as far as we have any documentary evidence, from the importation of Wood, Sandys and Gooking in and after 1620.

These horses came from England, and were obviously descendants of that particular line of English blood which soon was to be crossed to make the Thoroughbred.

Well, before the Revolution, however, in the administration of William Robinson of Rhode Island, Spanish horses directly imported to that colony from the old world were found to possess speed, and were both raced against and mated with the Virginia horses.

The only blood of the Conquistador horse used before the Quarter Horse went to Texas came from catching likely-looking wild horses that had worked up from Florida, and was doubtless limited to exceptional specimens of the weaker sex purely as a matter of economy.

Cullum's dicta on conformation strike any ear familiar with the sound of scientific approach, whether that of a horseman or not, more like wishful thinking than straight deduction from the breeding laws to which he professes to swear.

He says "know what you are breeding for." If you are

breeding for speed at the quarter-mile, then those horses who hold the quarter-mile records, according to the laws of evolution, must be possessed of that conformation best adapted and specialized to dash running.

If their withers and shoulders are slightly different (or feel and appear so on account of their great thickness) from those of Thoroughbreds adapted to running longer distances, one should draw only the conclusion that one type of shoulder is required for the dash, another for distance. (That the Thoroughbred cannot compete with the Quarter Horse at a dash even Cullum admits.)

Do the shoulders of Paddock even faintly resemble those of Cullum's Cunningham?

His remark that the Quarter Horse has only one merit is a far cry from his earlier rhapsodies over him. No horse is shorter coupled, another prerequisite to dash work. No horse is more nearly described as really having a leg of the right length under every corner. A development resulting from his evolution in an environment of standing starts and stake-turning races.

Likewise, an environment in which he had to rope-bust animals of much greater weight than his own, gave him exceptional thickness, which in turn makes him pack more weight per hand of height than any other breed or runner.

Is it any wonder that a horse typically weighing 1,100 at a height of 14.2, with a fork nine or ten inches clear inside his forearms, with the steep and high hindquarters especially evolved for standing starts, looks different in the shoulders and withers? Experience tying steers to both types of withers (and I have tied to grandsons of The Porter) in rough country (often going down hill) leads me most firmly to believe that the Quarter Horse type has survival value not only for him but also for his rider.

Were not the Major's rough rides and hard falls on and from Quarter Horses due to uncalculated speed and unexpected sensitivity to the rein? One can no more "sit" a good Quarter Horse cow pony on an English saddle when turning his best than one can a top flight Quarter Horse leaving the starting line. Whoever saw a Quarter Horse jockey even try to get one off without some solid "aids"?

A Quarter Horse with a good "reinda" can easily be thrown flat if judgment is not used.

Quarter Horse men generally know toward what end they are breeding. The small track, the rodeo infield, and the cattle range are his best markets since polo became modernized. Constant competition on the track; fifty yards around a stake and back; cutting weaner yearlings; roping calves and goats are the real proof of the pudding as to whether or not the breeder has intelligently conducted his operations.

Were he breeding for the Army exclusively, Cullum's preconceived picture of idyllic conformation (not necessarily related to reality) would doubtless be a more profitable practice. The Quarter Horse breeder's business, however, is founded on a purely utilitarian concept of aesthetics.

And in this State of Colorado I feel fairly sure that the

few Quarter Horse breeders are now turning better profit with this limited market than are the *many* users of Remount stallions who supposedly have the hunting and polo fields, the big-time tracks and bridle paths in addition to sell to, but who so often in reality experience some trouble in even unloading on the Army at $165.00.

I grant that the Quarter Horse is not adapted to the hunting field or the mile track. I grant that he is no longer adapted to the steady 35 miles per hour wide-turn style of polo played today. (But it is common knowledge that he used to fill the bill closer than any other when it was a game of almost 45 miles per hour spurts and swap-end turns, mingled with much slow scrimmage.)

But as just a riding horse it is ridiculous of Cullum to condemn so versatile a breed. His breed is first among dashing, starting, and turning horses; first in at least that intelligence required for range work; first in what it takes to work either at high speed in a "jackpot," or all day in rough country where changes cannot be made.

What does Cullum require in a "Riding Horse"? As large a percentage of Quarter Horses have easy gaits as of other breeds. And that their withers are too thick for any saddle but the western type I am sure will be denied by most of the many who have worked them under English, surcingle, and bareback. On one of them you know you have something betwixt your knees!

The rest of the Major's article, however, knowing Quarter Horse joints, etc., and denying that Westerners who ride rough country everyday all day for bread know anything about such deep (?) matters, cannot really be taken very seriously.

Most of these Westerners have also seen many "big-boned, deep-bodied, intelligent, strong, useful-looking Thoroughbreds," and grant them undisputed right to lord it in the hunting field and on the mile road. Most of the large scale ranchers have by now tried them, and tried admittedly good ones. Compared to good Quarter Horse stallions, they recently have been made as accessible as choke cherries.

But almost invariably too small a percentage of their colts combine both the physique and the intelligence required by the work, and the Major's admitted Quarter Horse high prepotency is sadly missed. A few Thoroughbred colts can be trained like circus horses even for rodeo work, but ask the man who owns one, and he will generally tell you that his horse is not a personality or "real hand." He admits to riding just a high-geared machine, and is limited accordingly.

Too often Thoroughbred colts have proved to have "power" as uncontrollable as that of "a Joe Louis," to have the "speed of a Glenn Cunningham," which can really get to town but cannot catch a cow if she is within fifty yards of a thicket, to have the metaphysical abstraction of "an Einstein," very disconcerting when tied hard and fast to something on the prod, and to have the "tenacity" to bumble himself through just like "John Bull," truly enough, but to have little regard for whether he rim-fired or hung-up his rider some place back in the brush.

"Short-Horse" Men

By BOB DENHARDT

THREE of the best-known "short-horse" men who were living during the turn of the last century, the heyday of the "Short-Horse," were William Anson, S. Coke Blake, and Milo Burlingame.

Uncle Billy Anson, as he was fondly called by his thousands of friends and admirers, was one of the first and greatest of important Texas Quarter Horse breeders. The youngest son of an English nobleman and distinguished in the official circles of the British Empire, he decided to seek new worlds, and came to Cristoval, Texas, in 1893 and began ranching. His friend, Dan Casement, once said of Anson: "He identified himself completely with his unaccustomed surroundings; and although he never abated in the slightest degree mannerisms in speech and behavior more usually encountered in fashionable London clubs than in Texas cow towns, he had by virtue of his square shooting and upright qualities, the liking and respect of a wide circle of friends among all classes of people."

At the outbreak of the Boer War, Anson bought Texas horses for the English Government. His judgment was so good that by the close of the war he had sold over 22,000 head. It was during these years that he acquired the nucleus of his superb band of Quarter mares. His first important Quarter stallion was a colt sired by the original Rondo.

In 1895 Anson began to play polo again in Texas, the

game he loved so well in England. Prominent among the friends with whom he played polo were two ranchers of Brady, Texas, who also were interested in polo horses, namely, Savage and Conover. In 1892 they all went to Cedarhurst, Long Island. Anson took his own ponies and played on the Rockaway team that year.

In 1902 he purchased the best sire of polo ponies he could find in England. The horse was imported by Eben, Jordan and Hamlin of Boston. Although not a "clean-bred" horse, he was seven-eighths pure. To Anson's disappointment the stallion was a complete failure. Later he bought from England another so-called polo pony stallion. This horse was the best two-year-old of his year and was called Senior Wrangler. This horse was not in the studbook either, but was seven-eighths Thoroughbred. Again he had no success.

In 1907, seeing that the horses he bought in the East were not successful, he again purchased a Quarter Horse stallion, this one sired by Arch Oldham and out of a Rondo mare. In 1908 he purchased Harmon Baker, a Peter McCue colt. In 1910 he purchased Sam Jones, the great Texas running Quarter Horse that had defeated so many Thoroughbreds. (See illustration of Harmon Baker facing page 86, and Sam Jones, facing page 135.)

When the Livestock Coliseum was built in Fort Worth and the Fat Stock Show was instituted, Anson was invited to become a director and to organize and take charge of the day horse show, and he continued in this capacity for about eight years. It was during this time (1906) that the first Quarter Horse class was held at the Fort Worth Exposition and Fat Stock Show. The first Quarter Horse show was judged by Professor F. R. Marshall, head of the Department of Animal Husbandry of Texas A. and M. College (see illustration of Coliseum, facing page 87).

All during his life Anson raised Quarter Horses, and many of the best Quarter Horses in Texas today carry the blood of his string. Anson was not satisfied in just raising Quarter Horses. He also studied them and their history, and on numerous occasions took the opportunity of writing about them.

S. C. ("Coke") Blake has been an outstanding Quarter Horse breeder for many, many years, and during that time has established a record for raising some of the fastest "short-horses" in Oklahoma, and also has gained national recognition for establishing a strain of Quarter Horses known as the Blake horse. The Blake horse gained its greatest renown in Oklahoma, Western Arkansas, Southern Missouri, and Kansas. The famous old race horse man of Peggs, Oklahoma, Smal Baker, said even though he had trained and run Quarter Horses all his life, White Lightnings, Steel Dusts, Cold Decks, and many others, the Blake horse was the fastest and most sensible.

Blake had the opportunity of crossing several very fine Quarter Horse strains, namely, the Cold Decks that came from Carthage, Missouri, the White Lightnings that came from the Alsups farm in Tennessee, the Brimmers from Illinois, and the Bertrand from Tennessee. Coke says the Blake horse got his beauty and style from the Bertrand, his muscle and intelligence from the Brimmer, his early speed and conformation from the Cold Decks, and his head and swiftness from the White Lightnings.

Coke Blake's idea of the perfect Quarter Horse was formulated in the 1870's when it was his privilege to see the original Cold Deck at Van Buren, Arkansas. Coke decided that if he could raise horses with the ability and intelligence of the Cold Decks, combined with some added style and refinement, he would have his ideal. Cold Deck's owner at that time was Foss Barker, who claimed his horse was the fastest animal on the globe. Coke reckoned he might have been, because people had just about given up trying to prove otherwise. Over the door to his stall, wherever he was, hung a large sign reading "Cold Deck Against the World!" So many people were ready to put money on Cold Deck that they would run him for a "nip of corn" or $10,000.00. Cold Deck stood a scant 15 hands, weighed 1,175, and was a dark sorrel. Cold Deck was foaled at Carthage, Missouri, and was supposed to be a son of Steel Dust, the horse that was to make such a name for himself in Texas. Foss Barker told Coke that Cold Deck was sired by Steel Dust and that there was a story connected with it. One day while Steel Dust was racing he was left in the care of a groom while his owner went out of town. The groom immediately got into a poker game. One of the players had a mare which he wished to breed to Steel Dust, but Steel Dust's owner had given orders that he was not to be bred under any circumstances. Soon Steel Dust's groom had lost all of his

LOBO
The great Quarter Horse stallion belonging to J. F. Hutchins of Pierce, Texas. There is a picture of this horse in action facing page 22.

LITTLE JOE, JR.
Little Joe, Jr. was champion Quarter Horse at Tucson in 1941, and ran his quarter in 22:3. He was sired by Joe Bailey (Gonzales) and his dam was sired by Little Dick. He is owned by Larry Baumer of Utopia, Texas.

RIALTO

Rialto is the well-known Billy Sunday stallion of Kendleton, Texas. Billy Sunday was by Horace H. and out of Carrie Nation.

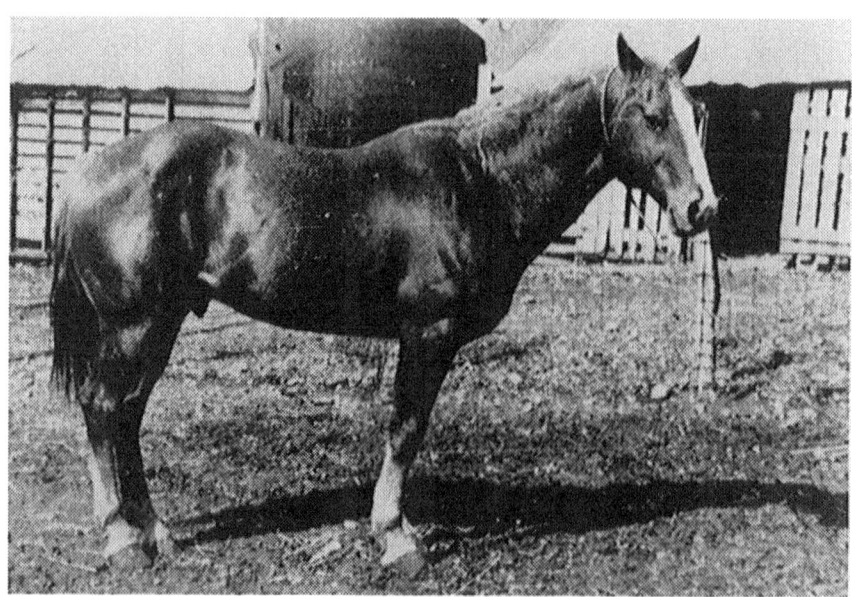

JOE BAILEY OF GONZALES

This Quarter Horse stallion is about the grandest old sire of all Texas. He was sired by Traveller, and his dam was by Old Joe Bailey.

money and had promised to allow Steel Dust to be secretly bred. The colt that was later born bore the tell-tale name, Cold Deck.

Blake began raising Quarter Horses in 1897. One of his first moves was to go to Wendell, Tennessee, where he knew a good son of Cold Deck was located. He succeeded in buying this son of Cold Deck and named him Young Cold Deck (see illustration facing page 199). Young Cold Deck had been raised by Joe Berry of Mount Vernon, Missouri. With Young Cold Deck, Blake raised his greatest stallion, Tubal-Cain. Tubal-Cain weighed 1,440 pounds, stood 15.2 and wore a double-0 shoe. His dam was a Brimmer; she stood 14.1 and weighed 1,200 pounds.

The story of how Coke knew he had raised a great horse is most interesting. One day a rain storm came up unexpectedly and he heard his horses running for the barn. Coke got up and went outside and by the time he could see the barn they were all inside. He could hear one shaking himself and it sounded like distant thunder. An old race-horse man from Missouri had told him once that whenever a horse shook himself and it sounded like thunder, that was a truly great running horse. So Blake ran to the barn to see what horse was making that noise. When he saw them it was the horse-colt Tubal-Cain. Blake said Old Tubal-Cain had "the eye of an eagle and the step of a deer."

According to Blake, Foss Barker, who owned and ran Cold Deck so long, was a real race-horse man. One match race with Barker was enough for Blake. One day, years after their first meeting, an Indian came to Pryor, Oklahoma, where Blake was living and raising horses, and wished to match a race for 350 yards with an old work horse he had. Coke, who had just harvested his cotton crop, decided to match the Indian for $500.00. He said, "I told my wife that if I lost the $500.00 we would plant another crop." However, they didn't have to. When Blake found the Indian at the edge of town, who should be with him but the old man, Foss Barker. Coke said, "I knew then that here was a race horse so I didn't match the race. It proved to be a right smart move, as some other town folk found out."

The high regard with which the Blake horse is held is ably shown by the statement of Major Grove Cullum, late of the Remount Service. "The Blake horse was developed by Mr. S. C. Blake of Pryor, Oklahoma, and I might say he is the best type Quarter Horse we have seen. In 1921 Mr. Blake presented the Remount Service with a Quarter Horse stallion called Tramp. Tramp was by Tubal-Cain, he by (Young) Cold Deck, he by Old Cold Deck, he by Steel Dust. The dam of Tubal-Cain was by Alsup's Red Buck."

Milo Burlingame is today one of the last of the rapidly disappearing class of "short-horse" men: men who used to live on, for, and from Quarter Horses. Milo was born in Canadian, Texas, about the time of the Civil War, but is today living and working in Albuquerque, New Mexico.

When visiting with Burlingame one day, the conversation drifted rapidly to Peter McCue, one of the greatest of all "Short-Horses." Milo said, "Sure, I knew Old Peter, he was the fastest horse I ever rode. That was back in 1892 or 1893 in St. Louis, Missouri." When asked how he was so sure of the date (Peter was supposedly foaled in 1895) he said he knew that was the date because on his trip north he went through the Cherokee strip and saw the waiting string of wagons. The thing that made the occasion stick to his mind was one wagon which had painted on its sides, "In God we trust, in Kansas we bust, let 'er rip, we're bound for the strip."

Milo at this time was traveling with a string of running ponies and on the trip had several horses with him, among them the famous Nellie Miller and Corn Stalk. He went first to a race meeting in Kansas City and then on to St. Louis. When he arrived in St. Louis Peter McCue was already at the fair grounds. Milo had a little difficulty in finding stable space that year, as there were 2,500 horses already located on the grounds.

Burlingame matched a few races and had considerable success with his Nellie Miller, which he considers the best horse he ever matched. (When he bought Peter McCue he was crippled and could not be run.) She was a "sure enough Quarter mare who happened to have a Thoroughbred dam." A salty two-year-old Quarter Horse colt had jumped a fence which separated him from an attractive young filly and had gotten her with foal without bothering to ask the owner for his consent. The mare was then considered undesirable and shipped to Canadian, Texas, and sold to Uncle Billy Miller, who had her when she dropped her foal. Burlingame bought the foal and called it Nellie Miller. Nellie ran the fastest quarter of her day in the Panhandle. Uncle Billy Miller later tried several times to beat Nellie with his horses but was unsuccessful. Milo chuckled and said, "Miller even imported a roan mare called Roan Jane from Missouri, but she didn't get the job done either."

Before Milo had run many races at St. Louis, he attracted attention. Frank James, brother of Jesse, was making the books at the fair grounds that year. He was matching a race between two of the best known "Short-Horses" of the day, Log Cabin and Sheriff. Frank had also caught Nellie Miller's time one morning and wanted to match her with the winner. This race, however, was never run.

It was Milo's success in riding Nellie Miller that brought him his chance with Peter McCue. One day after riding a winning race he was asked if he would ride Peter the next day, as there was some question about the jockeys. Milo did and with that ride grew his desire to own Peter. Several years later, after Peter McCue broke down, Milo had the opportunity to buy him. This he did and stood him at Cheyenne, Oklahoma, during the season of 1911. The accompanying picture (see illustration facing page 71) shows Milo holding Peter in the advertisement used by him to tell horsemen that Peter McCue was at service. Milo sold Peter McCue to Cy Dawson in 1915, who later sold him to Coke Roberds of Hayden, Colorado, in whose hands he died at the age of 28.

Some of the best horses Milo ever owned or raced were Sleepy Dick, Scar-Face Charley, Hay Seed, Grey Rabbit, and, of course, Corn Stalk, Nellie Miller and Peter McCue. Sleepy Dick, according to Milo, has a better record for the quarter than Bob Wade. Sleepy Dick was the most powerful horse he ever saw and made his record at Kiowa, Kansas. Peter McCue also is supposed to have run a 21-second quarter.

Milo is a small, slender man who carries his years like he was still a young man. Time has as yet made little impression on his physical or mental well being.

The day of the old "short-horse" man is about gone, but a new group of men are arising who will take the place of men like Anson, Blake and Burlingame, and continue in the path they laid out—to improve the Quarter Horse.

PART TWO

One Horse or Family

Billy Horses and Steel Dust

By J. FRANK DOBIE

"I OFTEN THINK that old Steel Dust must turn over in his grave when his blood is made responsible for some of the broomtails tacked onto him. It is still a name to conjure with, but almost every horse trader who has not recently joined the church or been rescued from backsliding will declare that his line of equine stock is largely Steel Dust stallions used in Texas, but for the most part that blood has gone into cow bunch outfits through grade stallions."—*A Ranchman's Recollections,* by Frank S. Hastings, 1921.

"Sam Bass liked the races so well that soon he wasn't content to remain a mere onlooker. He wanted to enter a pony of his own. Lacking the price of a good race horse, he cast about for a partner who might have a little money to put in with his. Such an associate he found in Armstrong B. Egan, usually called Army, a younger brother of the sheriff. Together, Army Egan and Sam bought a chestnut-sorrel mare from a farmer, Mose Taylor, who lived in the Hilltown neighborhood—later called Little Elm—on the McKinney road in the eastern part of Denton County. Sam had recognized the possibilities of this mare when he happened to see her tied near the courthouse. (This was about 1874.) She was two years old and about 15½ hands high. Her left hind foot was white above the hoof. She was said to have a strain of Kentucky blood through Steel Dust, a famous Texas race stallion of the fifties.

"Steel Dust was a Quarter Horse owned by Jones Green and Mid Perry at the southern edge of Dallas County, three miles below Lancaster. In 1856, people had gathered in Dallas from far and near to witness a Quarter race between Steel Dust and another celebrated horse called Shilo, brought from Tennessee by Jack Batchler. Eager for the start, Steel Dust reared and plunged in the chute. When he made his leap to clear the stall, he struck the wall and ran a splinter in his shoulder, disabling him. Shilo galloped over the track, and his owner claimed and received the forfeit. Steel Dust was blind from his injury and never ran again, but his renown was such that twenty years later it was a distinction to be able to claim Steel Dust blood for a race horse."—*Sam Bass,* by Wayne Gard; Houghton Mifflin Co., Boston, 1936.

"It is an old joke that every horse trader would earnestly affirm that his line of horses was largely Steel Dust in breeding. And old Steel Dust did leave some great sons in Texas and many cow ponies undoubtedly had his blood coursing through their veins. Yet grade stallions several times removed carried the Steel Dust blood into the cow ponies of most ranch concerns. Texas' greatest ropers and all-round cowboys preferred horses of the Steel Dust breed. There was Clay McGonigle, born in Texas in 1879, who for twenty years was one of the three or four top steer ropers of the world, who did his best roping on a Steel Dust horse. His choice pony was Rowdy, a dark brown horse of that breed, weighing around one thousand pounds."—*Bois d'Arc to Barb'd Wire,* by James K. Greer; Dealy and Lowe, Dallas; 1936.

The three quotations preceding show how conflicting traditions are regarding the origin of the Steel Dust horses, the blood which was once so pronounced on the ranches and race tracks of Texas. The following information I believe to be correct. It is furnished by O. J. (Onie) Sheeran, of Los Olmos Ranch, in La Salle County, and has been corroborated by George Clegg, of Alice. Both of these men have had a great deal of experience with horses and both have very concise memories.

Onie Sheeran says that his statements pertain to the Billy horses, but that the Billy breed came to be called also the Steel Dust and the Quarter, the Quarter Horse being bred to run a quarter of a mile.

Along in the 70's a gambler named Billy Blanton brought to Tampico, Mexico, from Spain, a dappled brown mare known as Paisana and a flaxy sorrel stallion named Whalebone. They were good runners but they did not save Billy Blanton from going broke gambling. He sold the two horses to William Foster, who was married to a cousin of Onie Sheeran's, and Foster brought them to Texas. This was in the late 70's.

From the pair were raised at least eight animals that proved to be very fast. "When I was a small boy," says

Sheeran, "I heard my father, Pat Sheeran, of Live Oak County, tell many times of these horses. He owned one of the colts called Chunky Bill, named for Billy Blanton, the original importer of the sire and dam. Also the general name, Billy, as applied to all the horses of this stock was probably after this Billy Blanton."

The oldest and most noted of the colts brought by Paisana and Whalebone was Rondo, a flaxy sorrel—sorrel with light mane and tail. He was purchased by Crawford Sykes, of Karnes County, who kept him and bred him until Rondo died. This stallion was such a superb animal and was such a vigorous breeder that he gave his name to a stock of horses—the "Rondo" horses—still remembered. Onie Sheeran owns today a grandson of Rondo. "I believe him to be," he says, "the best Quarter Horse in Texas." One of Rondo's sons that made a record racing was Little Jim, a Karnes County horse.

Three mares, all very fast, sisters to Rondo, were Blaze (a sorrel with a white face), Jennie and Kittie. Blaze and Kittie were sold into Mexico. Dow Sheley of San Antonio bought Jennie and raised some very fast horses from her, one of them being Little King, owned and raced by the late Dick Herring.

Four other horses from Paisana and Whalebone were Yellow Wolf, Pine Knot, Little Joe and Chunky Bill, already spoken of. These horses, also their sisters, Jennie and Kittie, were like their mother in color—a rich mahogany brown, dappled. In Galveston in 1886 Yellow Wolf and Chunky Bill raced a quarter of a mile for a wager of

$1,000.00, and Yellow Wolf won by a nose, his time being 21 seconds flat—the fastest time ever made by a Quarter Horse, says Onie Sheeran.

Little Joe was sold into Mexico for $50,000.00 and there won $25,000.00 in a race against his sister Kittie. Pine Knot was also sold into Mexico. What became of Yellow Wolf is not known.

Chunky Bill was owned by Bill Fleming of Bee County and D. F. Fox of Live Oak County before he passed into the hands of Pat Sheeran, who kept him until he died. His blood was well scattered over that part of Texas, and every man who got a horse from him boasted of his Billy horse.

These Billy horses—Rondo horses—Steel Dust horses—Quarter Horses—made their records as rodeo and ranch horses as well as for racing. Excepting in Mexico and here and there along the border there is no longer any Quarter racing, all the track men going in for Thoroughbreds. The polo people also are quitting the Quarter Horses for Thoroughbreds, except to cross them.

But hardy, short-coupled, level-headed, wonderfully adapted to the rein, strong, enduring and naturally savvying the ways of cow brutes, the Billy stock made the best of cow ponies. Straight Billy blood makes a fine ranch horse; mixed with old-time Spanish blood, it makes just as good, and some cow people think better. It is good to know that Onie Sheeran and many other ranchers are preserving this stock.

That the Billy and also the Rondo horses came to be

called Steel Dust horses there can be no doubt. Did the Steel Dusts have an origin apart from the mare and stallion imported from Spain by Billy Blanton? I am sure of the main facts about these Billy horses and am sure they came to be called Steel Dust horses, which were also Quarter Horses. But was there a separate Steel Dust line?

The South Texas Quarter Horse
By BOB DENHARDT

QUARTER HORSES, like other breed groups, have certain outstanding blood lines, and as may be expected, each traces back to some popular stallion. In Texas (and what is true for Texas is true for a great portion of the West) there seem to be just three great blood lines, established by three great stallions, namely, Shilo, Steel Dust and Traveller. Occasionally there arises in the descendants of these horses a stallion whose reputation and ability establishes a separate name and his get are in the future then known by this stallion's name. Such horses as Peter McCue, Harmon Baker, Ace of Hearts, Rondo, and Little Joe III are examples. It is sometimes forgotten that they belong to a larger and more important blood line. Some consider that Shilo was the greatest sire; others, Steel Dust. Steel Dust's blood was in Dan Tucker, the sire of Peter McCue, since his maternal grandfather was sired by Steel Dust. Steel Dust's blood was in the main stream creating the Billy Quarter Horse. J. Frank "Pancho" Dobie wrote an article for a magazine a few years ago entitled "Billy Horses and Steel Dust." After an interesting discussion of the Billy Quarter Horse he ended with the question: "But was there a separate Steel Dust line?" The answer, which he suspected, is no.

Each of the major blood lines will be examined in this article with something of the history of its more important horses.

The Billy Quarter Horses came from several sources: Steel Dust and Billy Fleming (who was undoubtedly a son of Steel Dust), Gallantry, Traveller, Paisana, and Whalebone.

The story of Steel Dust's arrival in Texas has been told many times, but the story of some of his close descendants who helped established the Billy horse should be mentioned. Grey Alice, Bill Fleming, and 80 Grey were Texas horses which were run around Sweetwater and Colorado City. 80 Grey was by Bill Fleming and out of a sister of Wolf Catcher. Bill Fleming was sired by Steel Dust and out of Grey Alice.

Will Morrison, who knew Steel Dust and had seen him run, said that he could run a Quarter in 22 seconds any time. Grey Alice was once clocked 21½. 80 Grey ran his first race in Colorado City in 1893 as a two-year-old. About the only horse to beat 80 Grey was McGonigle Roan, who was owned by the father of Clay McGonigle, the great steer roper. In Midland, 80 Grey successfully defeated the entries of two of the best "short horse" men in 1898 when he beat Dutch, owned by Jim Newman of Sweetwater, and Crawford, who belonged to Ellis Gardner of San Angelo.

The original Billy horse, according to Crawford Sykes and Ott Adams, was not the issue of Paisana and Whalebone (two horses imported by Billy Blanton and supposedly taking their name from him), but was from a horse called Billy brought from Kentucky by Bill Fleming to Gonzales County, Texas, just after the Civil War. The statement of Crawford Sykes is almost too authentic to question, as he was, according to most authorities, the greatest of all Billy horse breeders and the man who established the "Rondo" line of Billy horses. I quote from a letter written by Mr. Sykes: "The first I ever knew about Billy horses was about 45 years ago (approximately 1870) owned by Bill Fleming on the Guadalupe, near Belmont. . . . The old original Billy was the sire of McCoy Billie, and McCoy Billie was the sire of Rondo." Most of the early records show Billy was a son of Steel Dust. Ott Adams, who owned Little Joe III and Billy Sunday and knew these men well, also gives the origin of the name as Bill Fleming's Billy horse.

Crawford Sykes bred Arch Oldham, who was sired by Gallantry and bought by Mr. Sykes for one thousand dollars. Arch was a race horse from the word go and could run up to $5/8$ if necessary. Sykes considered Rondo the greatest sire of Quarter Horses "that ever was between the San Antonio and Guadalupe Rivers." There are men today raising Rondo horses who feel he was the greatest of all. One of these men, O. W. Cardwell of Junction, Texas, who owned Little Joe III at his death, says the Rondo family is the one that made the Quarter Horse famous.

PETER McCUE

Peter McCue was the greatest of modern Quarter Horse sires. He combined the Steel Dust and Shilo families, and his sons and daughters and their descendants rule the Quarter Horse world today. He was sired by Dan Tucker out of Nora M, a Thoroughbred mare. He was a freak horse, but he bred the right kind.

Peter McCue, Wt. 1430

Will make the season of 1911 at Cheyenne, Oklahoma.
TERMS: $25 to insure colt to stand and suck. Pasture will be furnished for mares coming from a distance at $2 per month per head. Extra fine mares will be given special attention, and if desired will be kept in stable, a reasonable fee will be charged for keeping. Notes are to be signed when mares are bred or taken away. Care will be taken to avoid accidents, but will not be responsible should any occur.

TOM CAUDILL, Keeper

MILO BURLINGAME, Owner
Cheyenne, Oklahoma

Although this statement is too broad, it does have some truth in it as far as South Texas goes.

The Traveller line, when crossed with the horses mentioned above, produced some of the best Billy horses. Traveller was bought by Dow Sheley in San Angelo, where Dow found him hitched to a fresno, building a tank for the railroad. This was at the turn of the last century. Some of Traveller's best colts were Texas Chief, Little Joe III, Joe Sheley, and El Rey. Traveller was just 15 hands and weighed about 1,300 pounds. George Clegg of Alice says he had the shortest back and biggest "pair of britches" of any horse he ever saw. He was a speckled sorrel and bred horses that had grey hairs in their tails.

Perhaps the Traveller line produced its best horses when crossed with the Rondo line. Rondo, raised and owned by Crawford Sykes, was bred to one of his own daughters, Old Mae, and from this union five great horses were produced. These horses were Little Joe II, who was sold into Mexico as a racer; Blue Eye; Nettie Harrison; Kitty; Baby Ruth, who later brought forth Paul El; and Old Jenny, who was the mother of Little Joe III. Rondo also sired Big Jim, who was to be the grandsire of Jim Wells. Old Jenny, sired by Rondo and out of Old Mae, got Little Joe III, one of the best known Billy horses of South Texas.

Little Joe III was bred by Dow Sheley and bought by George Clegg in 1905 when he was so small Clegg says he "could put him in a chicken coop." His wife wanted to know if he had to pay money for him since he was so little. Little Joe III outran Carrie Nation in his first race at the San Antonio fair in 1908. Clegg bought horses of the Shilo blood line from Watkins, who had Peter McCue and Dan Tucker at Petersburg, Illinois. He bought Hickory Bill, who was sired by Peter McCue, sight unseen, and also Lucrecio, the dam of Hickory Bill. Crossing these with the Steel Dust or Rondo line, he got some great horses. George Clegg, also called the Old Sorrel, owned by the King Ranch, and Paul El, who sired Spokane, who sired Lobo, were all his horses. Hickory Bill also sired Sam Watkins, who sired Coon Dog, ridden by Everett Bowman, and Dick Truit rides a bay sired by Sam Watkins. Little Sue and Old Tim, owned by Bert Benear of Tulsa, are Clegg horses. Pancho, outstanding Quarter stallion of Bill Warren of Hockley, Texas, is also a Clegg horse by Paul El and out of a Pancho Villa mare.

The other line of importance in forming the Billy horse is the Billy Blanton line imported into Tampico, Mexico. Blanton was a gambler, and during one of his reverses sold his two imported Spanish horses, a stallion called Whalebone and a mare named Paisana. Eight colts were raised from these animals. Jenny I, Kitty, and Blaze were the fillies, while Whalebone II, Little Joe I, Yellow Wolf (not the one belonging to the Waggoner outfit), Pine Knot, and Chunky Bill were the stallions. Crawford Sykes bought Whalebone and, crossing him with the get of Rondo and Arch Oldham, got some of the best horses ever sired in South Texas. Whalebone, Rondo, and Arch Oldham made Sykes the great figure he was.

Pat Sheeran, the father of Onie Sheeran, from whom

the following material in this paragraph was obtained, bought Chunky Bill and owned him until his death. Onie Sheeran, who used to jockey, spoke to the present author as follows: "I have ridden a good many fast horses in my life, but I believe that Chunky Bill was the fastest I ever rode, and I don't think a better one was ever raised. He and his full brother, Yellow Wolf, ran a quarter of a mile in Galveston in 1889 in 21 seconds flat, and Yellow Wolf won by a head only. I could mention many good race horses that I have known and ridden, but time will not allow. However, I cannot help but say something of the truest race horse that the sports ever knew, and that was Old Ace of Hearts, owned by Will Copeland of Pettus. He was not the fastest horse I ever knew, but the best. He won more races than other race horses, and he always did his best and was always ready when he was called upon. He was very quiet on a track as nothing ever excited him and he always did his best." Little Joe I was sold into Mexico for $50,000 and in one race against his own sister, Kitty, won $25,000.

The blood lines mentioned above all helped create the Billy Quarter Horse just as they created other great Quarter Horses not called Billys. It is surprising the number of great Quarter Horses arising from these same blood lines. The only important ones not known to trace to the above common families is Billy Anson's Jim-Ned-Brown-Jug line, later made famous by the Casements, and they may. Anson, like Clegg and the other great breeders, crossed blood lines to produce his greatest horses. Anson also bought Watkin's horses, purchasing a son of Peter McCue named Harmon Baker, and an Arch Oldham horse from Crawford Sykes which he named after the breeder, Crawford Sykes. This horse later was sold out to the Big Bend country to W. P. Fischer of Marfa. The Big Bend country also got the blood of several others of the great Billy horses, such as Ace of Hearts and Little Joe III. Ace of Hearts, when 13 years old, was on a bet unhitched from a wagon to run a quarter, and he defeated his challenger.

Mr. William Fleming, whose original horse Billy established the strain, and a neighbor of his by the name of John King, started a studbook for Billy horses at one time. Some of Billy's most famous sons besides McCoy Billy were Red Rover, Jim Brown and Midnight.

George McGonigle, father of Clay, who was celebrated as the champion steer roper of the world, moved from South Texas to the Odessa region and carried with him a stock of Billy horses. In later years, Rowdy, a Billy horse, made it possible for Clay McGonigle to set a world's record of 19 seconds for roping and tying a steer. According to H. T. Fletcher of Brewster County, who knew both Rowdy and Clay very well, Rowdy was almost human in the way he would take advantage of a steer. Rowdy belonged to Joe Gardner, a friend of Clay's. Joe tied a steer in 21 seconds on Rowdy at San Antonio. As coincidence would have it, Clay McGonigle died in Arizona in 1921 and Joe Gardner followed in a few months at Sierra Blanca, Texas. The two had roped thousands of steers on Quarter Horses and toured much of the world together.

We have a good description of the original Billy horse which belonged to Fleming, as described by a neighbor who knew both the horse and his owner intimately. He was a brown bay, 14½ hands tall, and weighed over a thousand pounds. His body was heavy but smooth, with sloping hips and legs comparatively short. His head was short and he had "fox ears" with a wide-set eye and sensitive nostrils. His neck was short and smoothly joined to his body. He must have looked much like his descendant, Lobo. This horse, Lobo (see illustration facing page 54) is one of the greatest Quarter stallions living in Texas, and is typically a Billy horse. He combines most of the great family lines. He goes to Shilo by way of Paul El, Hickory Bill, and Peter McCue. He goes to Steel Dust through both his dam and his paternal granddam, the first by way of Jim Wells, Rondo and Billy, and the latter by way of Crawford Sykes. Lobo is owned by Jack Hutchins of Pierce, Texas, but was bred and raised by Raymond Dickson, who owned Spokane until his death. There are few in Texas that have and know Quarter Horses as these two men.

There is strong evidence that the original Billy horse of Fleming's was a son of Steel Dust. This adds one more reason why Steel Dust is so justly famous. Most of the great horses bear some of his blood. One other fact that should be mentioned is the entrance of Thoroughbred blood into Quarter Horse strains. Of some forty-odd horses most often occurring in modern bloodlines, a third are known to have Thoroughbred dams. Undoubtedly other horses carried this blood. Some Thoroughbred blood of the right kind is an important factor in bringing these horses to their present status. Too much infusion of Thoroughbred blood, however, would change the conformation, and they would no longer be cow horses and "quarter of a mile running horses."

Billy horses, Rondo horses, Peter McCues, Travellers, all are Quarter Horses. They have been interbred so long it can no longer be said there is any pure line. They all have had their share of making the American Quarter Horse what he is today.

New Light on Old Steel Dust
By BOB DENHARDT

THE TEXANS had a horse, of which they were justifiably proud, as his equal in working cattle had never been bred. Coming to Mexico first with that bowlegged stockman, Cortés, the Texas horse had followed the Spanish cattle ever northward until he found what was a heaven for horses in the plains of Texas. For three hundred and fifty years these horses had been working with cattle, and when they reached Texas they were a race of animals capable of unbelievable feats of endurance and endowed with a cow sense seemingly inbred in the race. The Texans, typical horsemen, would bet their last shirt on the prowess of this horse, and the stage was all set for the appearance of Steel Dust, one of the best Quarter Horses ever bred.

There was found in Colorado, not long ago, the pedigree of an old Quarter Horse. This tattered and torn sheet (see illustration facing page 87), yellow with age, was advertising that famous old running horse, Dan Tucker. In the pedigree Steel Dust appears twice and the sire of Steel Dust three times. Steel Dust was by Harry Bluff, who was by Shortwhip and out of a Thoroughbred mare called Big Nance. The veracity of this pedigree sheet can hardly be questioned, as when it was printed too many people knew the facts and Trammell and Newman were well-known breeders who could not afford to be considered dishonest.

Of all the stories that have been told regarding Steel Dust, the following seems to be as consistent as any with the few known facts. When Texas had gained her independence she began to entice settlers by offering land free to incoming American homeseekers. In 1844 there arrived from Illinois a family by the name of Ellis. Two of the daughters were married, one to a man named Mid Perry. On the way to Texas they met some Virginians named Shelton, who continued with them to Texas. Both families had horses; among the bunch was a promising young dark bay stallion called Steel Dust, which belonged to Mid Perry. They settled south and east of Lancaster in 1846. The next year one of the Sheltons married one of the daughters of Ellis. Shelton died and his widow remarried one Alfred Bailes.

Alfred Bailes was a race horse man and brought horses to Hopkins County with him. In his string was the little dark stud called Brown Dick. Bailes had a rival in

Lancaster by the name of Jack Batchler. Bailes and Batchler had run a short race at Belton in 1856 and Bailes had won a sorrel mare called Queen. Batchler was now looking for a horse to beat Brown Dick and show his friend and rival he could also win a race.

The story now goes back temporarily to 1844, when we had left Mid Perry with a dark bay stallion which was a coming two. In 1857 this horse was being used by Perry as a saddle animal. He was thirteen, and although he had shown signs of great speed since he had been a colt, Perry had never raced him.

Batchler felt if he could borrow this horse and train him he might beat Bailes' Brown Dick. Perry, although unwilling, loaned Batchler the horse, and the training started. From here on I quote from a member of the family.

"In the fall of 1857, two miles west of Lancaster, Jack Batchler and Alfred Bailes staged the race. The unbeatable Brown Dick went down in defeat, beaten by an unknown horse 13 years old, who had just run his first and last race. After the race, Alfred Bailes sold Brown Dick to Jack Bridges of Hopkins County for $2,500 in gold, so Brown Dick returned to the place of his birth.

"After the race, Jack Lilley and a man whom we will call Lightfoot had a quarrel over the race. Lightfoot backed up. That night after Jack Lilley had gone to bed and was asleep, Lightfoot entered his room and shot him through the heart with the muzzle of the gun so close that there were powder burns on Lilley's underclothes.

"Mid Perry was so upset over the killing, which had taken place after the first race of the bay stallion, he never let him run again. The horse lived in peace and plenty until 1863 or 1864, and was then buried on Mid Perry's old place five miles southeast of Lancaster on the north side of Ten Mile Creek. So here lies the most talked of, written of, argued over horse with the least positively known origin of any that Texas ever had—the original Steel Dust of Texas.

"How do I know these to be facts? Thomas and Pollie Ellis are my great great-grandparents; William and Annie Shelton my grandparents. My grandmother married Mid Perry after my grandfather's death. Bob Batchler, a son of Jack Batchler, married Annie Smith, my second cousin. My informant is Henry Franklin Shelton, my father."

After Steel Dust beat Brown Dick at Lancaster in 1857, he became noted as a race horse. All of the participants were well known and the news of the killing spread it far and wide. Race horse men from the different counties within a radius of 200 miles of Dallas would pick out one or more of their best mares and breed them to Steel Dust. Notable among these men were the Files of Files Valley in Hill County, the Varnells of Ash Creek in Hill County, Tom Day of Seguin in Guadalupe County, Tom Haley of Johnson County, and Shelby Stanfield of Hood County, a race horse man of renown. Many others living as far as McLennan, Bell, Burnett, and on to San Antonio bred mares to Steel Dust. Frank Lilley bred a sorrel mare to

Steel Dust and raised a sorrel stallion colt that could run ⅝ or ¾ of a mile. "Wild" Jim Brown of Burnett County raised a sorrel horse that would run a mile. This horse was widely known in the late 60's and early 70's. His name was Old Rebel.

The chances are "Wild" Jim Brown is the same "Texas" Brown who later killed three policemen in Chicago when they tried to take his guns after a racing quarrel. "Texas" Brown turned up one year with a kangaroo horse with mutton withers that was the Man-O-War of his time. He cleaned up on every race. The following year he came through again, but this time nobody would race. They had learned better, so he bred his stallion to horses all over the country and left a trail of mutton-withered kangaroo ponies all over Texas. Jim Minnick of Crowell, Texas, says this did more to discredit the Quarter Horse than any other single item. He was a freak, and bred worthless horses, but his blood was left, and even today colts appear with his conformation. Brown was a bad man in Texas, killing several men, and when he took his horses to Chicago no one grieved and some said it was discretion. Having so many people looking for him he could not afford to give up his guns. He told the police in Chicago during the "ruckus" he would not give up his guns, then he turned and walked away. They started to stop him. He got three of them, but they got him, too.

One of the simplest stories ever told covering the origin of Steel Dust is the story told by Frank King. However, his tie-up with Justin Morgan has always seemed unlikely as the descriptions of Steel Dust and his colts bear but slight resemblance to the Morgan horse, and there is no reason to doubt Steel Dust's existence. The Steel Dust shown by the pedigree of Dan Tucker printed in this article could hardly be the horse told about by King, and to date it is the only document which bears any real authenticity and which gives any facts beyond refutation.

Frank M. King says, however, that,

"There was a Morgan stallion registered in the American Studbook in 1848 under the name 'Steeldust.' That same year Phil Buck, who ran around 15,000 head of Texas range mares on his ranch in the Matagorda Bay district of Texas, went to Vermont and bought a number of Morgan stallions from the Justin Morgan stock and turned them loose on his range. In a few years fast quarter hosses commenced to show up in the Buck herd and they were called Steel Dust."

Some writers claim Steel Dust was a Thoroughbred, others a Morgan, some an Arab, others a Barb. Certainly the Thoroughbred people have some claim, since his sire's dam was a Thoroughbred mare called Big Nance. By the same process we can undoubtedly eliminate all of the other breeds as having any close influence.

Steel Dust's running blood mingled with the Texas blood, and all of his urge to work with cattle, which had been recessive, came out in this new cross. Steel Dust and his get created a marked improvement on the conformation of the Texas cow horse, without detracting from his cow sense and stamina. The result was the best cow horse the Southwest had known. Now the cow horse of Texas has added weight and a fresh burst of speed without any loss of that intuitive cow sense which the centuries had bred in the Spanish horse.

We have no reliable description of Steel Dust, the horse which was one of the principal founders of the Quarter Horse strain in Texas, but the startling uniformity of his descendants gives us a rather clear picture of his appearance. Steel Dust animals can be told from any Quarter Horse just as readily as a Quarter Horse can be told from other breeds. Another important Quarter Horse family which exists today is the Billy horse. The descriptions above describe the Billy horse more accuratetly than they do the Steel Dusts. The Steel Dusts mount up better in the shoulder and withers with a better set to the neck. To the casual observer he might more closely resemble a compact Thoroughbred than would the Billy horse which might by the same observer be taken for a Morgan. Steel Dusts, however, do not resemble Thoroughbreds. Doubtless fanciers of both breeds would object to such a statement. Steel Dusts are shorter in the neck and shoulders, more compact and closer to the ground. The forearm of the Thoroughbred is not so heavily muscled. Seemingly the Steel Dust has more muscle on the outside of the legs, while the Thoroughbred is muscled more on the inside. Steel Dusts have the smooth and compact shape, short back, and deep barrel of the Quarter Horse, but the unusually heavy musculature which stamps the breed seems to reach in the Steel Dust a peak which "amounts to almost a deformity in his bulging jaw." This also explains why the Steel Dust strain is occasionally referred to as "Big Jaws." Anson termed it a "Coarseness of the head." Dan Casement says, "These massive jaws seem to serve as a fitting symbol of the tenacity and determination which mark the Steel Dust strain. They make a strange contrast to the alert little ears which denote the keenness of the horse's sensibilities, and furnish a substantial background for the forehead and eyes that bespeak deep stores of equine wisdom." Those who are acquainted with the Criollo Horse of the Argentine will see a striking resemblance in the two animals.

Steel Dust was undoubtedly the first Quarter Horse to make a marked impression on the cow horses of the Southwest. Other strains of the Quarter Horse, as well as different members of the Steel Dust family, have established branches of the Quarter Horse family in the Southwest. Some of the better known are the Steel Dusts and Billy horses mentioned above, Cold Decks, Printers, Rondos, Copper-Bottoms, and the Blake horse. All are offshoots of the main Quarter Horse family. The Blake horse is of the Cold Deck line of Steel Dusts and was developed by S. C. Blake of Pryor, Oklahoma. Major Cullum of the Remount Service has stated they are the best Quarter Horses he has ever seen. In 1921 Mr. Blake presented the Remount Service with the very good Quarter Horse he had raised called Tramp. Tramp was by Tubal-Cain by Cold Deck by old Cold Deck by Steel Dust. The dam of Tubal-Cain was by Alsup's Red Buck.

The earliest stockman to popularize the Quarter Horse was William Anson of Christoval, Texas. Billy Anson came from an aristocratic English family, and, like so many of the younger sons of the English nobility, came to the New World during the last half of the 19th century to seek his fortune. It is said that, although he became a real Westerner in the best sense of the word, he never lost his accent or English manner.

Anson got his first opportunity to collect Quarter Horses when he was buying horses for the British government during the Boer War. While gathering large numbers of horses, particularly of the Steel Dust type, he kept some of the best, and with these as a base, he began to breed them on his Head-of-the-River Ranch on the Concho. Perhaps the outstanding stud which he produced was Jim Ned. Jim Ned sired two very famous colts. One was Brown Jug (see illustration facing page 135), which was sold to the Correllitas Rancho in Chihuahua. Pancho Villa raided the Correllitas later and appropriated Brown Jug for his personal mount. Concho Colonel was the other well-known son of Jim Ned, and more appears on the Colonel below. Anson wrote several articles on the breed, being one of the first men to study the history of the Quarter Horse, and the blood of his horses is found in most of the Quarter Horse studs in the country.

Following Anson, Dan Casement, owner of the Juniata Farm of Manhattan, Kansas, became an outstanding breeder of Quarter Horses, favoring Steel Dusts. His first stallion was called Concho Colonel, a horse which later became well known in the Southwest. Casement bought the "Colonel" from Anson, his sire being Jim Ned, Anson's famous horse. Concho Colonel was a half-brother of Brown Jug. The "Colonel" was taken to Casement's ranch in the Unaweep Canyon, close to the Utah line. "Colonel" worked cattle and handled his *yeguada* of mares until he died at the age of 22. He left 139 foals, some being kept, but most of them going to owners throughout the country. Concho Colonel's colts were stamped with the typical Steel Dust conformation. So marked was this uniformity that Casement said he had never seen it equalled in any horse. Some of these colts gave good accounts of themselves. Fireball, foaled in 1914, out of a Thoroughbred mare, was several times champion polo pony at Santa Barbara while owned by Lafayette Hughes of Denver. Rosky, a year younger, foaled by a Texas cow horse (mustang-mare) not only played polo in France, but also was hunted on the Atlantic coast by Frederick Prince. Concho Colonel begot his best colts through Spanish mares.

Casement sold the majority of his horses after the war, but in 1923, through a partnership with Ed Springer of the CS Ranch of Cimarron, New Mexico, he continued breeding. With this partnership came mares with blood of the celebrated Steel Dust, Little Joe. Some of the more famous of his colts coming from CS mares and the "Colonel" were Coleen, which won the Grass Riders Grubstake at Fort Riley, and Clipper, medal pony of the 11th Cavalry Club of Monterey.

Concho Colonel was growing old and Casement began

looking for a fitting successor to continue the strain. He found the dam he wanted in a Walker mare, twelve years old at the time of purchase. Named Little Judge, she was by Little Steve out of Sal by Grey Joe, and, as Casement so aptly puts it, who could ask for a more mellifluous Quarter Horse pedigree? Balleymooney was the colt she produced by Concho Colonel, and he represents the best sire Casement developed. He lived 18 years, producing many fine colts. Deuce, who is still alive and at work for Casement, was one of Balleymooney's best sons. Two other outstanding sires from Balleymooney are Frosty and Red Dog.

Writing to the present author in 1938, Dan Casement said: "I still have my Steel Dust stud, the Deuce by Balleymooney. To him I breed every year three daughters of his grandsire, Concho Colonel, one of his half-sisters, a Thoroughbred mare and two granddaughters of Senator. With their progeny we work our cattle here. These are the only horses any cowman should ride."

Peter McCue, Wonder Horse
By BOB DENHARDT

QUARTER HORSE—The very word spells romance throughout the West. Any name which brings to mind such idols as Steel Dust and Shilo, Peter McCue and Barney Owens, or any of a dozen other wonder horses, could not but have glamour. However glamorous the name of Quarter Horse may be, he still is

GOLDEN CHIEF

Golden Chief is the great Copper-Bottom stallion of R. L. Underwood, Wichita Falls, Texas. He is the sire of Dexter, facing page 7.

HARMON BAKER

Harmon Baker was one of Billy Anson's great stallions. He was a son of Peter McCue. Many stallions throughout the Southwest today trace directly to this great stallion. Anson bred him during the season and raced him during the winter.

COLISEUM IN FORT WORTH

This picture of the First Quarter Horse Show is thought to be perhaps the earliest picture of a Quarter Horse show held in America. It was found amongst the possessions of William Anson and carries the date 1908.

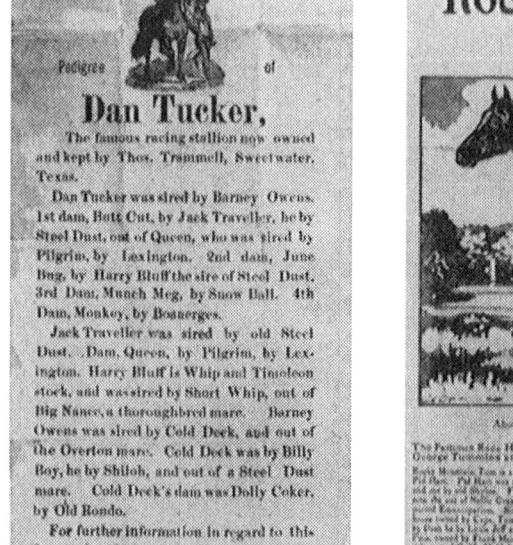

the top horse in the Western rancher's eye. He still makes the best cutting horse, the best roping horse, and the fastest saddle animal the world has seen.

Perhaps his greatest popularity in the past drew to a close some twenty years ago. Then for a period, while the Government was pushing Thoroughbred horses as remounts and relieving some of the strain of overproduction of the Eastern studs, his popularity waned. No Western horse raiser, if he lacked independent means, could afford to raise horses which he could not sell. The Government was the best buyer, but they would buy only half-breeds, preferably from their own stallions. Luckily a few of the real old-time Westerners could never forget the animal on whose back they and their fathers had gotten a start in life. Some of these men had the money to continue raising Quarter Horses.

Today the popularity of the Quarter Horse is returning with greater vigor than ever and ranchers all over the West are once again turning to the animal they love—an animal whose ability on the ranch, in the rodeo and on the short track has never been equalled. Just a month or so ago a Texas rancher had a Quarter Horse auction. Those who before doubted the popularity and pull of the very name Quarter Horse should have attended, for there arrived what proved to be one of the largest crowds ever to attend an auction of any kind in the Southwest, with representatives from all the largest ranches of the neighboring states on hand.

Every section of the Southwest has had its great Quarter Horse, a horse which has left a legend behind. Whenever horsemen gather, sooner or later the talk will veer to this or that great Quarter Horse, and his exploits will be enumerated. Texas is extremely fortunate in this respect. Texas has either been the home, or at least the stamping ground, of most all of the great Quarter Horses. If one were to draw a line from Sweetwater to Alice he would have springing up within a day's ride of that line many of the greatest short horses ever to develop in the entire West.

One of the greatest of all Quarter Horse sires was a freak horse called "Peter McCue." Today his blood runs in most of the great Quarter Horse studs standing in the West, and if a man possesses a mare descended from this great animal she is almost priceless. Peter McCue has been called the greatest horse that ever ran a short race. You could breed him to a box car and get a running horse. Although his name does not carry the halo which surrounds Steel Dust, Peter McCue was in every way just as great a horse. Certainly he is the greatest descendant of Steel Dust. Peter McCue had in his ancestors Harry Bluff, Steel Dust's sire, appearing three times, Steel Dust appearing twice, and June Bug, a half-sister of Steel Dust, appearing once.

Peter McCue's breeding explains in at least a partial fashion his tremendous ability. He was sired by Dan Tucker, that great animal brought out of Petersburg, Illinois, by Thomas Trammell of Sweetwater. Trammell also bought Dan Tucker's sire, Barney Owens, in Carthage, Missouri. Owens was not as large a horse as his illustrious son and grandson, weighing only 1,200 pounds and standing a short 15 hands. Dan Tucker was a little larger, standing 15.2 and weighing nearly 1,300 pounds. Barney Owens was sired by Cold Deck, he by Billy Boy, who in turn was sired by Shilo and out of a Steel Dust mare.

Peter McCue's sire was out of Butt Cut, who was sired by Jack Traveller, who was by Steel Dust. Steel Dust was sired by Harry Bluff, who was out of Big Nance (a Thoroughbred mare) and sired by Short Whip. Besides the Thoroughbred Big Nance already mentioned, Jack Traveller's (Peter McCue's granddam's sire) dam was Queen by Pilgrim by Old Lexington, all Thoroughbreds.

Dan Tucker went blind and was killed when he was accidentally allowed to get into the same pen with another stallion. Walter Trammell, the son of Thomas Trammell, says his father always considered Barney Owens, Peter McCue's grandsire, the greatest horse he ever owned. Trammell sold William Anson of the San Angelo area many of his best horses, particularly his Ace of Hearts, whose name was later to become so famous out in the Big Bend country. Harmon Baker, whom Anson bought from a man in San Antonio, was bred by Peter McCue.

Peter McCue, although he sired some of the greatest of all stock horses, was himself a runner, running short races in Texas, Oklahoma and the North. Sam Wilkins of San Antonio brought Peter McCue from St. Petersburg, Illinois, to Texas. He was 16 hands and weighed 1,430, and despite this size was the fastest horse ever to run on a short track. While in St. Louis he ran the fastest quarter mile ever run by a horse on four legs that was recorded by more than one witness with a watch in hand. When this time was made he was being ridden by Milo Burlingame. Three independent railbirds clocked him in 21 seconds flat—the fastest time ever made by any horse in a quarter. Since it was five o'clock in the morning and just a workout, it was not official.

Peter McCue's time was phenomenal, and he was a freak horse, as an examination of his picture in the pages of this book will show. However, other Quarter Horses have approached this speed. Bob Wade ran a quarter in $21\frac{1}{4}$ seconds at Butte, Montana, and Rainbow, by Senator, the Colorado horse ran a quarter in under 22 seconds, as also did Yellow Wolf in Galveston, Texas, in 1886.

Peter McCue after leaving San Antonio was taken to Oklahoma and while there bought by Coke Roberds, of Hayden, Colorado. Roberds then kept him and cared for him until he died at the age of 28.

Peter McCue sired many famous horses, but Carrie Nation, who at one time held the world's record for the $\frac{5}{8}$ mile, and Buck Thomas, who ran 49 races and won 48, are two of the best known runners. Most of his sons were kept as stock horse sires and his daughters are still famous as brood mares.

Trammell and Newman, who bought Peter McCue's sire and grandsire, operated around Sweetwater and were the great Quarter Horse raisers of that section of Texas. Jim Newman had a Quarter mare called Little Danger that turned in next to the fastest quarter ever run in El Paso when she ran one in a shade over 22 seconds. He also raised Callise, and Pan Zareta, a full sister, which was the only horse to run a quarter in 21 seconds plus at El Paso. Walter Trammell still keeps one of Pan Zareta's horse shoes. She was sired by Abe Frank and out of Minyon, who was out of one of the famous Charles Haley mares, which were in turn sired by Ran Cocus, a Thoroughbred. Jim Newman gave Walter Trammell a wonderful Quarter Horse called Booger Red. He would run up to $7/8$ of a mile and stood 14.3 and weighed 900 pounds. He was lost in a selling race at Los Angeles and bought by Pinkerton of detective fame, who used Booger the rest of his life as a stud at his Colorado ranch.

In the San Angelo area the great name which has come down as a Quarter Horse breeder is Billy Anson. However, there were breeders in that district before Anson. One of the first Quarter Horse men was Alex Gardner, who came from Zavala County to the San Angelo area in about 1882. He was famous particularly for two great stallions, Pancho and Joe Collins. Gardner kept a thousand dollars posted at all times to any comer in the quarter mile, but Pancho never lost a race. Pancho was always fat. They could not keep him worked down. Whenever someone wished to race and took a look at Pancho they decided it would be easy money because he was so fat. He was always sweated and drawn before a race and was one of the meanest horses ever to wait for a starter's signal. Gardner finally had to build a chute to start him in.

However, once the start was given, Pancho was gone. It was claimed he never ran a race in over 22 seconds. Anson got some of his best blood from this Pancho horse. Pancho was probably a Billy. Jim Ned is supposed to have come from Pancho. Jim Ned sired Brown Jug, the horse which was sold to the Correllitas Ranch in Mexico and later appropriated by Pancho Villa as his favorite mount. Jim Ned also sired Concho Colonel, later owned by Dan Casement, whose get is still taking top honors in horse shows in Arizona, Colorado, California, and Kansas.

The blood of these early horses still runs in modern Quarter Horses. Let us examine only two centers where top Quarter Horses may be found today and see how the blood of these great old stallions is still producing the best.

First, Wharton County, Texas, where some of the best may be found. Jack Hutchins, who is operating the old Shanghai Pierce Ranch, owns Lobo, which was given to him, I believe, by that grand fellow, Raymond Dickson, who knows and loves Quarter Horses as few people now alive. Lobo is one of the outstanding Quarter Horse stallions in the Southwest, and carries the blood of the greatest in his veins. Lobo was sired by Spokane, Dickson's great horse. Spokane in turn was sired by Paul El, who was by Hickory Bill, who was by Peter McCue. Thus, in Lobo's blood runs Dan Tucker, Barney Owens, Cold Deck, Steel Dust, Shilo, and many other famous names. The Duncans of Egypt also have horses with this same breeding, one of their best stallions being Major, which was also out of Dickson's Spokane. W. A. Northington of the same county has a stallion called Lucky Strike who goes back to Peter McCue by Hickory Bill.

In Arizona there is quite a Quarter Horse center around Willcox, with W. D. Wear and J. E. Browning being the two best known. Browning owns Billy Byrne, which is a real ranch horse that would rather rope and cut than eat. He has never taken worse than second in a show, and was the Grand Champion cow horse at the Tucson show in 1939 and first in Sire and Get in 1938. Billy Byrne was sired by Dan Casement's Balleymooney, who was by Concho Colonel, who was by Billy Anson's old Jim Ned. Wear owns not only Tony, which has taken first in both the Phoenix and Tucson shows, but also Frosty, who goes back to the old Anson stock. Anson horses, as shown before, were related to Peter McCue through Anson's famous horse, Harmon Baker, often misspelled Hiram Baker. Harmon Baker was a son of Peter McCue.

So many times nowdays you hear the statement made that Quarter Horses are great but they are not raised now like they used to be. They are slow. That is just where the mistake is made. There are just as good Quarter Horses raised today as ever. However, they are not publicized, nor do they have Kentucky Derbies to cause the man on Main Street to talk about them. With racing outlawed, they have in many cases been kept only on the ranch and in the rodeo. The rodeo has done more to keep the tradition alive than any other single activity. Most of the great roping and dogging horses have carried Quarter Horse blood. Talk to any of the "Turtles" and get them to tell you about this or that great roping or dogging or pick-up horse and you will start talking Quarter Horses.

Today there are men in all the Western states raising Quarter Horses. To name just a few of the outstanding horses there are all through the West that have not already been mentioned, one might start with that game little horse, Buddy, which recently won the short race at the Lafayette horse show in California. He ran 3/16 in a little over 14 seconds, carrying 116 pounds, including a stock saddle, and he is just 14.1 hands and weighs only 970 pounds. He is owned by Dunnigan of Yuba City. Red Cloud is another great Quarter Horse in California, located at Victorville. Jack Casement in Colorado and his father in Kansas both raise top Quarter Horses. Marshall Peavy of Steamboat Springs, Colorado, owns a mare called Margie (see illustration facing page 183) which is just about the fastest mare in all Colorado, and Coke Roberds of Hayden always has good Quarter Horses. In his day he has owned both Peter McCue and Old Fred, and he still raises their get. Max Yates at San Saba, Texas, has a descendant of Anson's old Brown Jug, called Billy, which has great possibilities, and he is out of a mare which still bears Anson's old brand. There is a negro named Taylor in Kendleton, Texas, who has a dark sorrel stud called Realto (see illustration facing page 55) out of old Billy Sunday, which is one of the great sires of South Texas. Warren Brothers of Hockley, Texas, have some good "Quarters." Pancho (see illustration facing page 181), a dark brown horse which goes back to Peter McCue by way of Paul El, and Alasan, a grandson of Old Ace of Hearts, are probably their best. Lee Underwood of Wichita Falls has probably more uniformly good Quarter Horses than any other single man in the country, and in the present writer's opinion (with the possible exception of his Golden Chief), Dexter (see illustrations facing pages 86, 7) is his best stallion, although still too young to be proven a really great breeder. Howard Hampton of Clarksville raises some good ones principally sired by Joe Hancock (see illustration facing page 102), the horse Tom Burnett called the greatest Quarter Horse that ever lived. Duwain Hughes of San Angelo also has some good Quarter Horses.

Anybody who has a little time and energy can find Quarter Horses being raised all over the country and in all the Western states. Today they are becoming more popular and demanding higher prices than ever before. In the not too distant future the breeders will organize and create a horse association and studbook. After all, they are raising a horse whose breeding goes back before the Thoroughbred, a horse whose blood was liberally utilized in the creation of all the modern American saddle breeds. It is only to be expected that this great horse will have its day. Only the independent spirit of the Western rancher has delayed such an organization in the past.

The Great Little Horse Billy

By HELEN MICHAELIS

THE BILLY FAMILY of the Quarter Horse was named after its founder, William B. (Billy) Fleming, who was born in Georgia November 18, 1830, and came to Texas in an early day by way of Mississippi. He joined the U. S. Rangers' force on the Texas frontier and was in many Indian fights. He was a Confederate veteran and served throughout the duration of the Civil War. In 1865 he settled at Belmont, Texas, where he founded and established the Billy Horse in 1866 with Old Billy and Paisana.

The original Billy Horse was small, compact, heavily muscled and fast. The most common colors were brown and sorrel and the brand carried by those raised by Billy Fleming was the Ace of Clubs. As a result of a wounded right arm received in the Civil War, Billy Fleming could not write; therefore he kept no records of his horses. The only written records are the few he dictated to those who requested them for horses purchased. With his left hand Billy Fleming signed the pedigrees. One of these records witnessed by Paul Murray was given December 27, 1907, at Capote Farm, Guadalupe County, to the late Fred Matthies, and was the pedigree of Little John Moore (alias Jack). In one corner of the pedigree was written: "This is a correct pedigree. W. G. Fleming. Witness, Paul Murray. A Billy Horse raiser for 30 years. Originator of the Billy Horse family since and in 1866."

Old Billy, the foundation sire of the Billy Horse, never

ran a race in his life. He was foaled about 1860 in the vicinity of Belmont, Texas. For the duration of the Civil War he was chained to a tree. In 1866 Billy Fleming bought him for $500.00. His hoofs had grown so long it was necessary to saw them off; his neck was bruised and bare from the chain and never grew hair again. Old Billy was by Shilo, a son of Union and Shiloa, and out of Ram Cat, a daughter of Steel Dust and Fanny Wolf. Shiloa was a daughter of Old Shilo, foundation sire of the Shilo family. Old Shilo was by Van Tromp by Thomas Big Solomon by Sir Solomon by Imp. Sir Archy (see illustration facing page 119) Imp. Sir Archy was by Imp. Diomed by Florizel by Herod, out of Imp. Castianira by Rockingham by Highflyer by Herod.

Steel Dust, foundation sire of the Steel Dust family, was by Harry Bluff, a son of Short Whip and Big Nance (Thoroughbred mare). "Harry Bluff is Timoleon and Whip Stock." Timoleon was by Imp. Sir Archy.

Paisana, spelled "Pysiano" by Billy Fleming, was a little seal brown mare owned originally by Oliver and Bailes, south of Seguin, in Guadalupe County. Oliver and Bailes were partners in raising Quarter Horses before the Civil War, and when they dissolved partnership, about 1866, out of Oliver's part Billy Fleming got Paisana. Billy Fleming won a number of races with Paisana. She was a 350-yard mare but could run a quarter of a mile. Paisana was by Brown Dick, a son of Berkshire (Bailes' Berkshire, sire of Fanny Bailes) and out of Belton Queen, a daughter of Guinea Boar and Missouri Gal.

Brown Dick was matched in 1865 against Queen, owned by Jack Batchler of Lancaster, Texas. Bailes won the race and also Queen. This Queen was probably Belton Queen, the dam of Paisana.

In the fall of 1857, two miles west of Lancaster, Alfred Bailes ran Brown Dick against Steel Dust, which Jack Batchler had borrowed from Mid Perry. Steel Dust, 14 years of age, won the race. After the race Bailes sold Brown Dick to Jack Bridges for $2,500.00 and Brown Dick returned to the place of his birth. After Billy Fleming let Anthony go he got a Steel Dust stallion called Rondo. He was a small, heavily muscled sorrel horse. He was old when Fleming got him and he was branded all over. His breeding was unknown, and with him Billy Fleming almost ruined his horses.

Shilo, by Anthony and out of Sweet Lip, was a dappled bay and could outrun his half-sister, Fashion, 350 yards. He was owned by Tom H. King, Belmont, Texas, who was at one time Fleming's partner. Shilo was stolen and gone almost a year. When he was recovered he had been gelded; a few months later he was sold to a Mexican and went to Mexico with ten or twelve other King horses, all of which were Fleming stock.

Fashion foaled in 1887 and was a brown mare that stood about 14.3. She was bred by Tom H. King and was out of a four-mile mare King got from Kitchens near Eagle Pass, Texas. Fashion was a full sister to Lemonade and made the circuit with her and Yellow Wolf (raised by Joe Mangum, but Fleming stock) under Trainer Wade

McLemore. Fashion broke the record for ⅜ of a mile at San Angelo, Texas, when she ran it in 34 seconds. She beat the champion of Mississippi for ⅜ of a mile in the 90's. She outran Blue Jacket, by Lock's Rondo, ¼ of a mile. She was registered with the Jockey Club as: by Whalebone, out of Siltenn. August 15, 1891, Fashion ran ⅜ of a mile at Lampasas, Texas, in 34 seconds. Red S. made the same time in 1896 at Butte, Montana. This record was lowered in 1924 when Airflame ran ⅜ mile at Santa Anita in 33 seconds. The record today for ⅜ mile is 32-4/5 seconds, made by Galley Slave, a two-year-old, in 1938, at Arcadia, California. In her old age Fashion was used as a brood mare. She was the dam of a sorrel filly, Lemon, owned by Fred Matthies, Seguin, Texas; a filly by the Thoroughbred, Morgan Scout, that went to Mexico City, and a colt that went East.

Lemonade foaled in 1888 and was a full sister to Fashion. John Bouldin said she was the fastest 500-yard mare in the world. Lemonade was registered in the Jockey Club as a bay mare by Whalebone and out of Silvereen. February 21, 1893, Lemonade won a race of 4½ furlongs at New Orleans, Louisiana, in 57 seconds. She was carrying 91 pounds and won by two lengths. At the time she was run under the name of McLemore & King.

Pink Reed, a stallion, by Anthony and out of Sweet Lip, was bred by Billy Fleming. Mr. Jack Hardy came from Mississippi and bought Pink Reed to beat a Mississippi mare. Within two weeks Mr. Hardy returned and said Pink Reed had foundered and wanted another horse. He asked Billy Fleming if he had anything that could beat the Mississippi mare. Billy Fleming told him Alex Gardner, a half-brother, could beat any horse in the world except Pink Reed. Alex Gardner was a stallion also and was the same age as Pink Reed. His dam was Artie, a daughter of Old Billy and Paisana. Mr. Hardy borrowed Alex Gardner and took him to Mississippi. He beat the mare and was sold at the end of the race.

Little John Moore (alias Jack), a stallion bred by Billy Fleming, was by Anthony and out of Little Blaze. He was bought about 1907 by Fred Matthies. Among the colts sired by Jack was Coley, a black horse bred by R. C. Appling, Kingsbury, Texas, out of a Billy Fleming mare. Coley sired Cricket in 1927. Cricket is now owned by Ollie Crawford of Gonzales, Texas, and is the dam of Spencer and Teddy Bear, full brothers, by Joe Bailey, which is a great great-grandson of Old Billy on his sire's side.

Billy (Dribbel) was a black baldface horse bred by Anthony Dribbel. He was by Anthony and out of a four-mile mare owned by Anthony Dribbel. Billy was purchased by R. T. Nixon and was the foundation sire of the Nixon strain of Quarter Horses. He sired the Nixon mare that was the dam of the mare, who was to be the dam of the horse, Joe Bailey.

Jenny Oliver was a black mare by Old Bailey and out of Paisana. In the late 80's, shortly before he quit racing, Billy Fleming took her and four sisters and brothers overland from Belmont to a race meet at San Angelo, Texas. Three of the other four were Dora, Alice and Rover. The story goes, Billy Fleming always hit a race meet broke but left rich. He was broke when he reached San Angelo and before he could raise sufficient funds to pay rent on the log stables, he was obliged to prove his horses were fast. He chose Jenny Oliver, a 22-second mare, and after she had run Fleming had no trouble getting loans. All his horses won the races in which they were entered; Jenny Oliver won two, one against a Pat Garrett horse. Alex Gardner bought the others and took them to the Indian Territory, where he sold them.

Little Brown Dick, son of Old Billy and Paisana, was raced all over East Texas by Ruff Herring. He was "borrowed" from Billy Fleming and never returned, but was taken to the Indian Territory and sold. The little brown horse branded Ace of Clubs may have sired some fast colts out there whose sire was recorded as: "breeding unknown." In Texas, Little Brown Dick sired the dams of Little Ben and Aury. Aury was bred to Little Ben and the resulting foal was Susie McQuirter, the dam of Old Joe Bailey. Old Joe Bailey was bred by Dick Baker, Weatherford, Texas. He was a bay Quarter Horse, foaled in 1907, and died in June, 1934. He founded the Joe Bailey family and some of the best get were Joe Bailey (dam of Joe Bailey, the Nixon horse), Old Yellow Wolf and Dan (sire of Jimmie Allred, see illustration facing page 166).

Little Blaze, by Old Billy, out of Paisana, was a sorrel mare with flax mane and tail. The Carrigan boys of Beeville bought her from Fleming when she was a two-year-old. They raced her and when she broke down Fleming bought her back and used her as a brood mare. She was the dam of Little Joe Moore (alias Jack) by Anthony.

Joe Collins was a dark brown horse and foaled about 1883. When he was a three-year-old past, Alex Gardner bought him from Billy Fleming. Joe Collins ran as a two-year-old, but got too heavy to run. He was later owned by Clay McGonigle. Joe Collins sired Blue Gown, out of Gray Alice; Buckshot, out of a Thoroughbred mare, and Sis, out of a McGonigle mare.

Pancho was a light brown horse foaled in 1884. When he was a two-year-old past, Alex Gardner bought him from Billy Fleming. Mr. Gardner paid $1,500.00 for Pancho, Joe Collins and Dora, which were full brothers and sisters. Pancho was not as good a sire as Joe Collins, but he was a great little race horse. He was open to the world and it is said he never lost a race. He could outrun Traveller a quarter. One of his trainers was J. J. Armstrong, brother of D. C. Armstrong, who is B. B. Van Vactor's trainer. Pancho stuck a nail in his foot and died of lockjaw about 1890. The best known of his colts was Jim Ned, sire of Brown Jug and Concho Colonel, which made Billy Anson's Billy horses famous throughout the United States. Brown Jug went to Mexico and it is said he was stolen by Pancho Villa. Concho Colonel passed into the hands of Dan Casement of Kansas and lived to be over 20 years of age. He sired Balleymooney, Fireball, Coleen, Clipper, Rosky and about 135 other colts that also did credit to his name. Balleymooney sired Frosty, Red Dog, Billy Byrne and others.

TONY

Tony is the Quarter Horse stallion owned by W. D. Wear of Willcox, Arizona. He is almost the perfect type Quarter Horse, and is about the closest approach we have to the early colonial type short distance running horse. He was sired by Possum (King) and out of a Bulger mare.

JOE HANCOCK

Joe Hancock is the famous stallion owned by the T. L. Burnett Estate. Joe Hancock is a grandson of Peter McCue, and was seldom beaten for a distance of a quarter of a mile. He is getting the best running colts on the short track today.

WHIMPY

Whimpy is No. 1 horse in the registry of the American Quarter Horse Association. He was the blue ribbon horse at the Fort Worth Exposition

McCoy Billy, by Old Billy, was the sire of Sykes' Rondo. Sykes' Rondo, bred by Sykes and Mangum of Nixon, Texas, was a chestnut horse with flax mane and tail and stood about 15.1. He foaled about 1869 and was the foundation sire of the Sykes horses. Sykes' Rondo sired Jenny II (dam of Little Joe III), Baby Ruth (dam of Paul El), Big Jim (sire of Katy M.), Little Joe II (a gelding that went to Mexico), Nettie Harrison, Kittie II, Blue Eyes and many more good horses.

Besides Little Joe III, Jenny II was the dam of Black Bess and King Cardwell (alias King and Possum).

Little Joe III, bred by William and Dow Sheley, Alfred, Texas, foaled in 1905 and was sired by Traveller. Little Joe III was a rich dappled mahogany, stood about 14.2 and weighed between 950 and 1,000 pounds. He was owned by the Sheleys 1905-1906; by George Clegg, 1907-1911; by Ott Adams, 1912-1926; and by O. W. Cardwell, 1926-1929. In 1929 Little Joe III, 23 years of age, crippled himself in a chute on the Cardwell Ranch near Junction, Texas, and was destroyed. His get were too numerous to mention, but a few of his colts that are well known throughout the state were: Nita Joe, Joe Moore, Rainbow, Clear Weather, Zantanone, The Northington Horse, Plain Jane, Ada Jones, Grey Mare, Adaline, Mamie Jay, Little Sister, Poco Bueno, Pancho Villa, Clementia Garcia, Jim Wells, Pat Neff, Cotton Eyed Joe, Lupite and Lady Love. (See illustration of Little Joe III facing page 199.)

Black Bess, by Warrior, was the dam of Cotton Eyed Joe and Little Hickory Bill's dam.

King Cardwell, known better as King and as Possum, was sired by Traveller and was bred by Dow and William Sheley, Alfred, Texas. When Dick Herring of Devine, Texas, got him he was known as King, and then John Kennedy in South Texas got him and called him Possum, and it was only recently discovered that he was the same horse as King. Of King's get in Texas, probably the most widely known is Joe Bailey. Possum's get in Arizona include Guinea Pig, Baby King and Red Cloud.

Bob Wade was foaled in 1886 and set the record of ¼ of a mile when he ran it in 21¼ seconds at Butte, Montana, August 20, 1890. "Goodwin's Turf Guide" shows Bob Wade, in 1890, won 14 races out of 25 starts. He ran in Texas, Montana, Oregon and Colorado.

Crowder was the famous race horse that outran Mayme (Minnie) Sykes in San Antonio, Texas. He was ridden by Oliver Parmer and owned by the Johnson Brothers of Hondo City, Texas.

Among other horses raised by Billy Fleming were Mayme B., Fraud, Jim Crumby, Joe Murray and Crawford.

Crawford is said to have been sired by Old Billy. He was taken to the San Angelo country by Jack Boone, brother-in-law of Alex Gardner. Crawford was a fast horse, but he lost races to Dead Cinch, Mayme (Minnie) Sykes, 80 Grey and Judge Thomas.

The Billy Horse has developed into one of the strongest families of the Quarter Horse, principally because Billy Fleming timed his horses and bred only the fastest ones.

It is said he raised lots of 22-second horses and never raised a complete failure. His secret of success was to not breed a Quarter Horse to a Thoroughbred to get a fast short distance horse. He believed the Quarter Horse was a distinct breed; that he contained no Thoroughbred blood, and was of Spanish-Barb origin.

About 1888 Billy Fleming quit racing, but he continued to raise and sell horses. By this time his horses were scattered all over the United States and the Republic of Mexico. One bunch of eleven head which he sold to some Mexicans for $40,000.00 were lost in a chicken fight the night they reached Mexico. What eventually became of those horses is yet to be learned; but the Billy Horse in the United States found a way to many tracks.

In 1907, Billy Fleming, at the age of 77 years, sold the last of his Billy stock, six mares and Little John Moore (Jack), to Fred Matthies, Capote Farm, Seguin, Texas, and followed them there, where he lived until his death, April 30, 1911. He was buried in the Matthies family cemetery and with him were buried many unwritten pedigrees of his horses. Mrs. Fred Matthies and Mr. John Bouldin, two of Billy Fleming's surviving friends, have made possible the recording of the true history of one of the greatest little horses that ever lived—the Billy.

PART THREE

Quarter Horse History

The Oldest Distinct Breed

By WILLIAM ANSON

I DO NOT WISH to exploit any breed, type, or individual of my own creation or conception, but I bring to notice a true race of horses which possess claims to be considered the oldest distinct breed in the United States today. First let me discuss the established type and the historical origin of the Quarter Horse; secondly, let me describe him as he exists today, and forgive me if I am obliged to introduce a personal element. I have been in close contact with these horses as an admirer for the past twenty years and as a practical breeder since 1899, and my observations are to a certain extent the result of my own experience.

The meager historical facts which I present are the result of casual inquiry, but not of systematic research, and doubtless much valuable information could be secured from old colonial papers and documents. In reference to Mr. Ogilvy's remarks about the horse breeding experiments of our government, I am reminded that at one time I made advances to the Department of Agriculture with the idea of inducing them to take the matter up, and by inquiry and research pave the way towards establishing a Quarter Horse studbook; but they were too busy with the new breeds they themselves proposed to create, buying gray draft mares in England, or drawing up specifications for the American carriage horse. "Very much interested in your account of the horses, glad to have further information," was the burden of their reply, but no offer of practical assistance; and as I had neither the time nor the means to do the work myself, I dropped the matter.

In *The Horse of America,* by Wallace, we find the following description of Quarter Racing, written by J. F. D. Smith, before the Revolutionary War:

"In the southern part of the colony and in North Carolina, they are much attached to quarter racing, which is always a match between two horses to run one quarter of a mile, straight out, being merely an exertion of speed; and they have a breed that performs it with astonishing velocity, beating every other for that distance with great ease, but they have no bottom. However, I am confident there is not a horse in England, nor perhaps in the whole world, that can excel them in rapid speed, and these likewise make excellent saddle horses for the road."

Notice the definite statement, "they have a breed." This description of Quarter Horses and Quarter Racing might very well have been written by a casual visitor in 1910 instead of the middle of the 18th century. I have not established historical connection between these old colonial Quarter Horses and those to which I next make reference; this article may catch the eye of someone who could throw some light on the subject. My next point in claiming that the Quarter Horse has long been known as a distinct and separate breed is the fact that the American

Studbook recognizes the indebtedness and origin of some of their pedigrees to Quarter Horse families. In its second volume there is a list of stallions whose ancestry was necessary to tabulate the foundation pedigrees for Bruce's studbook, and among these we find "Cherokee" Quarter Horse; he was the sire of several stallions whose blood runs in many American Thoroughbred families. Although he is the only one I found in the list described as a Quarter Horse in black and white, there is no doubt that many of the other stallions of unknown pedigrees in this volume were of the same breed. His presence there, however, described as a Quarter Horse, without other qualifications, proves that Bruce himself knew and recognized the breed. That eminent authority, Hamilton Busby, told me that he knew little about Quarter Horses beyond the fact that they entered largely into the pedigrees of American Thoroughbreds, especially those originating in Illinois. There are some curious facts as to the extent this has happened in recent years.

There is little doubt in my mind that the superior soundness and constitution of the American Thoroughbred is owing in some measure to the infusion of this short distance racing blood. While it may not have improved their class in long distance racing, it certainly has not detracted from their value in other ways; old Sam Harper was one of the best mile horses of his day, and his dam was a Quarter Horse mare. Anyway, the athlete who can do his 100 yards in ten seconds or better is admired as much as the mile champion.

Owing to the absence of a studbook these horses have undoubtedly been bred perhaps more for type and performance than for strict blood lines and pedigrees. Comparatively few can lay claim to pure lineage, but in spite of this the type is very firmly established, and with whatever breed he is mated the Quarter Horse transmits certain unmistakable racial characteristics to his offspring. There are, however, a number of established pedigrees known to the old Quarter Horse racing men, which could be obtained were any effort made to establish a studbook. Many modern winners on the American turf have been bred directly from Quarter Horse dams in the second generation; and many so-called Thoroughbreds are much more closely allied to the Quarter Horse family than this. An example of the legitimate Thoroughbred-Quarter Horse cross was Charlie Wilson, raised by John R. Nasworth, near San Angelo, about 1889. Racing in his breeder's colors, I believe he was never beaten up to three-quarters mile, and subsequently passed into other hands, he gained notoriety in a scandal on a Chicago track, was ruled off the turf, and afterwords won when and how he pleased at Guttenberg and other outlaw race courses. He was sired by the Thoroughbred Buck Walton, and his dam was out of a mare of Quarter Horse breeding by a Thoroughbred stallion.

A more recent example is Arch Oldham, by Imp. Gallantry, bred along the same lines and also registered "for racing purposes only." He is now about eight years old and has been at the stud for the past four years on the ranch of Crawford Sykes, a noted Quarter Horse breeder in Southwest Texas. He has been doing a big season in the summer; then has raced very successfully every fall and winter. In outward appearance he resembles a Quarter Horse more than a Thoroughbred. I am now using a three-year-old stallion sired by him out of one of Mr. Sykes' old Rondo mares, which is thus five parts Quarter Horse and three parts Thoroughbred. As showing his adaptability to range use, I have not written thus to extol the Quarter Horse as a racing machine, but to prove that he has a distinct character of his own which could not have been acquired except by very deep breeding.

Following advice on my arrival in Texas in 1890 I invested in some mares and a stallion of a breed and type that did not suit this country. In 1899 my four and five-year-old geldings were sold for $10.00 a head, and I was glad to get them off my grass at that, being determined to change my methods or go out of the horse business. While interested in polo, and in close touch with polo pony dealers, I had noticed the beautifully shaped animals from Quarter Horse stock, sometimes in Texas called Steel Dust horses, in the same way some trotting horses are spoken of as Hambletonians. Steel Dust was a brown horse of unknown breeding, possessing very marked Quarter Horse characteristics. He was stolen from Tennessee during the war and proved a very successful sire of short distance speed. These ponies were all of the same stamp and many were of marked excellence, proving that there must be something beyond chance in their consistent make-up and performance. Several good pony mares were in my stud in 1899, and I traded off a few mares for good Quarter Horse mares, and bred the balance to a good Percheron stallion which saved me from utter loss in the original investment. In subsequent years I was in every nook and corner of Texas buying horses for the British Government, and acquired every strikingly good mare I came across until I had about sixty head. Moving farther West, I selected that part of the country from which I had drawn my best purchases and fitted up a horse ranch.

My first stallion was the best available, and the use of him with other stallions of the same breed, and also two high-class English polo pony sires, has more than ever convinced me that in his own sphere the Quarter Horse is without a peer. He has quality combined with weight, marvelous bone and substance. His disposition is good and his great endurance is conceded by those who have used him. He is fitted for the work in view. All my winter ranch work is done on my stallions. These horses have to be grain fed in any case, so that I kill two birds with one stone. As soon as the breeding season is over I turn the stud horses loose in the stallion pasture, while the younger ones run the year round, and treat them like a bunch of saddle horses. They come up morning and evening for their feed, and all of them, except one or two of the older ones, are fed together in troughs in the open lots. I never put a horse in a stable if I can avoid it. Old Jim Ned, my first sire of this breed and now eighteen years old, still does more ranch work in the winter than any horse on the place. To quote from Mr. Ogilvy, these Quarter Horses are "bred from the same or similar stock as are actually engaged in the service required." Many of the remounts during the Boer War had a good proportion of this blood, and the official Blue Book reports issued by the British Government and summarizing the results of the Remount Commission inquiry, show in what high esteem they were held on active service in South Africa.

Distinctive features are a marvelously strong back and loin, immense muscle, especially in the forearm and gaskins, great weight to inches and good feet and legs. The stallions especially have very heavy jaws, and are apt to be thick or coarse in the neck, the head being sometimes set on at rather an acute angle. If they have a fault as a breed it lies in this and in the fact that they are apt to have rather heavy shoulders, which, however, generally ride well and do not give an uncomfortable feeling in a downhill gallop. I am sure Mr. Ogilvy will agree with me that a horse like Brown Jug, which stands under 15 hands and weighs 1,125 pounds, is from his shape eminently fitted for mountain work. They have a deep girth and are wide across the region of the heart. The muscles behind the shoulders make them easy to stick to in an English saddle or bareback. Closely and deeply ribbed, they have big bellies without being paunchy. They are kind and intelligent. They give good service in harness either on the road or to the plow.

It may sound strange that this breed of short distance racing horses should have the build and qualities essential to successful ranch use. Their conformation is the result of many decades of breeding from race winners, and the type has been accentuated as it has proved its merit in these two and three-furlong dashes. The almost universally placid disposition is explained by the fact that a mean-tempered, flighty or nervous horse is at a discount on the quarter mile track. Many such races are won or lost on the start, and many starts under the curious rules and terms agreed to in these matches would occupy hours. The object of each jockey was not only to get the best of his opponent on the jump-off, but also to wear out the temper and strength of the rival horse. The pony which could keep his temper under these very trying conditions and at the same time hold his nerve and muscular power under such perfect control that he was always ready to shoot away at the word, then after one of the many false starts pull up and quietly return to the post, had a very large winning percentage in his favor.

It may also sound strange that the existence of this breed of ponies has not been more generally known and recognized. As a racing pony the demand would always be limited to a narrow section; as a polo pony he has been appreciated, but here again the demand is limited. Why then has he not been more widely used for range purposes? Up to 1900 there appeared to be an inexhaustible supply of cheap ponies, and, under conditions described by Mr. Carpenter at the beginning of his letter, they were so plentiful and so cheap that no one dreamed of a shortage. Up to the past year or two most ranches have been working with their old mounts, and when they discover that their horses are too old for the work of many more summers, they find that, turn where they may, the horses they could formerly buy by the hundred have ceased to exist. When Mexico and Arizona horses were going at so much the dozen it was waste of time and money to breed one's own cow horses. Except in old Mexico the racing days for the Quarter Horse are about over, but he may yet find long-delayed recognition as a national breed and he will supply a want on our Western ranches.

The above article explains to a certain extent my reasons for launching into the breeding of Quarter Horses. The class of animals I was raising in the 90's was not only losing me money, but the enterprise was of little interest to me personally, and it struck me that if I was to continue in this line of business I might at least produce an animal which would be of pleasure to me, at the same time being of use in the general conduct of my ranch. The more I have inquired into the matter, the more evidence I obtain that the Quarter Horse has been bred on distinct lines, both as to speed and conformation, from the time when we have first mention of him. There is no race of horses in the world which mark their offspring more indelibly and no sire will transmit his qualities in a more thorough fashion. Any man conversant with the breed will detect its influence even in the second generation. Jim Ned, my original purchase, is a beautiful brown horse, about 14.3, and weighing about 1,100 pounds. For twelve years he has served me faithfully, out in the pasture during the summer months with his mares, and the remainder of the time in the saddle horse pasture, doing as much or more work than any cow pony on the ranch; he is a true representative of a great race. Even tempered and intelligent, easily kept, never ailing or sick for a day, sure-footed and never known to be guilty of a mean act or trick, this is the horse which has laid the foundation of my stud. The young stallions I am now offering were all sired by him. The two other stallions in service, Sam Jones and Crawford Sykes, were, it is needless to say, selected with the same object in view; they are being bred principally to mares sired by old Jim, as he is affectionately known on the ranch; their colts from the polo-bred fillies are not reserved for stallions. My Head-of-the-River Ranch is devoted to the development of the Quarter Horse; I have dedicated all my attention and resources to this interesting problem for the past ten years, and I am convinced that I am producing a horse which will fill the want of the Western ranchman, or any man who wishes to breed an animal which will be equally useful as a cow horse, buggy horse, and, if necessary, farm horse—a horse which is perhaps even more appreciated when taken to New York or other Eastern points, whether used for riding, driving, or for the game of polo.

[*Some day, perhaps, someone who loves Quarter Horses will give Texas A. & M. an endowment dedicated to the development of the Quarter Horse. There could be no more appropriate State than Texas, and few locations better than Anson's Head-of-the-River Ranch on the Concho.*—The Editor.]

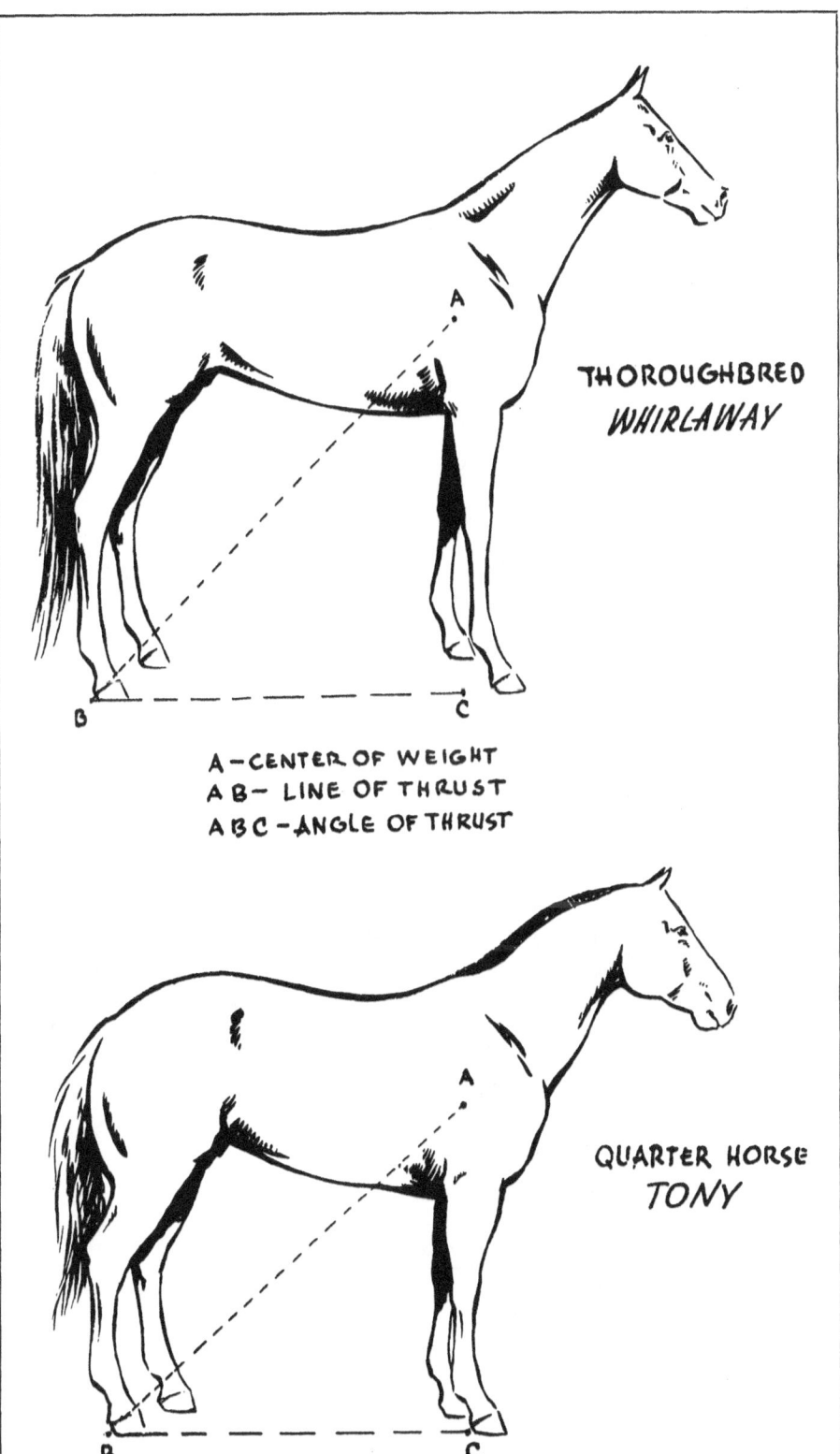

SIR ARCHY

According to Helen Michaelis, who is one of the authorities on Quarter Horse Blood Lines, the Quarter Horse owes more to this imported horse than any other early sire, with the possible exception of Old Janus.

QUARTER RACE IN MEXICO

This race shows the historic race between the Texas bred Ginger Rogers and the Mexican bred La Gaviota, run in Vera Cruz recently. Ginger Rogers won. She is owned by Sr. J. D. Raines of Mexico City.

Quarter-of-a-Mile Running Horses
By WILLIAM ANSON

FEELING more than grateful to my friend, Dan D. Casement, for the kind references made to me in his article "About the Quarter Horse" in *The Gazette of* April 27, I am naturally reluctant to correct one mistake which he makes in quoting me as saying that "The Quarter Horse undoubtedly traces back to the Thoroughbred race horses imported from England."

My conclusions, drawn from the little research work that I have engaged in, are that the Quarter Horse was a distinct breed in early colonial days, prior to the time when the English Thoroughbred could have had much influence on colonial breeding. I am aware that this point of view is not regarded with favor in certain quarters.

It is not a matter of personal opinion; it is formed on the authority of statements to be found principally in Wallace's *Horse of America, Frank Forrester's Horse of America,* by Henry Herbert, and Edgar's *Studbook.*

Facts, as stated in these works, furnish proof that in colonial days there existed a breed of horses called "quarter-of-a-mile running horses." We know that the abbreviated name, Quarter Horse, originating in Virginia and the Carolinas, drifted through Tennessee, Kentucky, Ohio, Illinois and across the Mississippi River, and was brought to Texas, with specimens of the breed itself, by early settlers. The description of the colonial Quarter Horse applied to the Quarter Horse as we find him today.

The following passage, read many years ago and quoted in full, from Wallace, induced further investigation:

"J. F. D. Smith made an extensive tour of the colonies, especially of Virginia, before the Revolutionary War. In speaking of quarter racing he says: 'In the southern part of the colony and in North Carolina they are much attached to quarter racing, which is always a match between two horses to run a quarter of a mile, straight out, being merely an exertion of speed; and they have a breed [I wish to call special attention to this positive statement] that performs it with astonishing velocity, beating every other for that distance with great ease, but they have no bottom. However, I am confident that there is not a horse in England, nor perhaps in the whole world, that can excel them in rapid speed.'"

In *Frank Forrester's Horse of America* there are numerous interesting references to the Quarter Horse.

The most conclusive proof of what they are, and the influence that the Quarter Horse must have had on the early American race horse, is to be found in Edgar's Studbook, only one volume of which was completed. There is possibly a good reason why it was not carried on. It is rare, and few copies seem to be in existence. On the title page we find the following passage:

"Containing the pedigrees of the most celebrated horses, mares and geldings that have distinguished themselves as racers on the American turf from one-quarter of a mile up, and from which have descended the most valuable blooded stock at present in the United States."

This was about the year 1832. In this old and original studbook with its quaint wording we find more than 40 horses and mares specifically described as a celebrated or famous American Quarter Running horse, or mare.

In several instances there is a full description of size, conformation and interesting accounts of races won. This of itself might not substantiate the claim that the original American race horse was in any way indebted to these old Quarter Horses. Bruce, whether he used Edgar's Studbook or not, inserted 36 horses or mares, described in Edgar's Studbook as Quarter Horses, but (with the exception of two) failing to credit them with the said prefix, "C.A.Q.R. Horse or Mare." Bruce assuredly did not insert any animal in his earlier volumes without good reason or reasonable assurance that the then existing families of American race horses (such as could not show authenticated pedigree) had some of the blood of these horses in their veins. I have known several old race horsemen in Texas who were personally acquainted with Bruce. I have heard them say that he himself was an ardent admirer of the Quarter Horse.

In taking up the question of Quarter Horses tracing back to imported horses, the Quarter Horse always has been and always will be a composite breed, with a mixture of Thoroughbred blood. In early days, however, the only imported horse which seems to have had much influence on the breed was a horse called Janus. From all accounts, and the number of Januses which appear in old pedigrees, he must have been nearly as prolific as our old Texas Steel Dust, undoubtedly the most prolific horse that ever stood on four legs.

Janus, while imported, was not in the English studbook, and his pedigree was never authenticated. Herbert says that he was supposed to be by a certain Old Janus, tracing back, of course, to the Godolphin Arabian; his dam was only "reputed to be." His immediate progeny were only good for short distance racing. I have found six horses by the name of Janus in Bruce's Studbook.

Henry Herbert, in Volume 1, page 145, says: "Janus produced the fleetest then, and since, known as Quarter Horses."

It is known that long distance racing became more popular and fashionable as years went by. Knowing human nature, it is not hard to realize how pedigrees tracing to imported horses would be more thought of than those showing evidences of this Quarter Horse blood. Had I been diligent enough to record all I have been told, I could give yards of pedigrees of Texas Quarter Horses. I have heard a dozen different accounts of Steel Dust from men who knew him, all differing except in one particular, and there is little doubt that he came from southern Illinois, the home of many well-known "short-horses." My own stallion, Harmon Baker, very successful in his younger days in quarter-mile and three-eighth races, and most successful as a sire, came from the same locality.

On page 128, *Frank Forrester,* Volume 1, the writer, in questioning the statement that before the importation of Fearnaught (about 1764) there was little beyond quarter racing in Virginia, goes on to say, "It is only to be understood in the case of second-rate racers that quarter running was in vogue at this period." I have quoted enough to prove the existence of the Quarter Horse as such in the colonies.

We claim that men acquainted with the Quarter Horse as he is today find that he has retained the distinctive qualities which he possessed in early days, and that, when bred, stamps his individuality on his offspring, as a Quarter Horse, no matter what he is bred to, this in spite of the fact that he has been denied the privilege of a studbook to guarantee his parentage. He has undisputably been bred for type, perhaps more than for pedigree.

I should like to say a word of appreciation for the good work of the Remount Association, co-operating with the Remount Department. It is impossible to overestimate how much this move is affecting the intelligent breeding of riding horses. The liberal and sane methods employed, up-to-date and reasonable, will have a wonderful influence on the American riding horse of the future. Speaking for myself, I can only say that through this means I now have the use of a stallion to continue my breeding operations, in which I have been engaged for more than 20 years—a horse which I could not find myself, though I had been searching and inquiring for some time for such an animal. This is only one of many instances, and its effect has been not only to supply many needed stallions, but to put life into an industry which was nearly defunct.

Importance of Racing and the Remount
By GROVE CULLUM

To GAIN a true picture of the Western horse today it is necessary to go into the background of which he is a product. And this is a versatile one. He draws his inheritance from a long and varied line; from those first horses brought in by the Spanish conquerors; from the very first importations of our Eastern horses, harness horses and Thoroughbreds.

This mixed clan of which the Western horse is composed was molded in the hands of farmers, plantation owners, sportsmen, pioneers, fur traders, cattlemen, Indians, outlaws and sheriffs. The inheritances passing through and molded by these various hands have mingled together in equally varied terrain, from the salt marshes of the Gulf Coast to the mountain peaks of the Rockies. He grazed and migrated with the buffalo in the great grassy plains; he eked an existence from the semi-deserts of the Southwest and grew wild in the foothills of our mountains.

The story of the Western horse is the story of the conquest of the American continent. I shall attempt here a brief outline of his origin, his growth and his development.

The first settlers to reach the Atlantic Coast brought no horses with them. They found a country devoid of trails and roads except for footpaths of the Indians. And the first migrators to move West traveled on foot and by canoe. Just when the first horses were imported I am not sure, but it is certain that these came several years after the first settlements had been established, and that they came principally from England and Holland. It is quite definitely established, however, that in the year 1645 there were about 250 horses of both sexes in Virginia. And in 1640 the New England colonists found they could afford to send some eighty horses to the Barbadoes.

Before the trails widened into roads, the saddle horse was the pioneer, the trail blazer so to speak, in the encroachment of the Eastern settlers on the wilderness of the Middle West. As trails broadened gradually into roads, the harness horse commenced to play the more important role in the lives of the settlers and in the ever-increasing number of Western pioneers. For it must be remembered that these early builders were not engaged in sport but in the stern business of wresting from the fields and the forests the bare necessities of life, and a harness horse could pull more members of the family, more of the implements necessary to the struggle, than the saddle horse could carry on his back.

So it was that there grew up in the Middle West vast numbers of horses bred for harness rather than the saddle. From these and subsequent importations there developed many families of strictly harness horses. The Morgans, Hambletonians, Cleveland Bays, French Coaches and Kentucky Whips are a few of the well-remembered strains. Little did one hear those days in the Middle West of the famous families of Thoroughbreds that today are such great factors in the improvement of the American horse.

As the colonies grew and as moderate wealth gave time for leisure and sport, many outstanding sportsmen directed their attention to the breeding and developing of flat racers. This was more particularly true in the Southern colonies—in Maryland, Virginia, and the Carolinas—where plantation life was developing in contrast to the small farms and manufacturing centers of the North. The first runners were "short-horses" very much on the type of the Quarter Horse whose influence is so conspicuous to this very day in our Western country. (In a later article I shall discuss the origin and influence of the Quarter Horse on our present-day Western horses, for he has played an important role.) About the time of the Revolutionary War, the Thoroughbred or the long distance racer commenced to replace the "short-horse" in popular favor in the East, and particularly in the South.

Thus while the vast numbers of harness horses were developing in New England, New York, Pennsylvania and the Middle West, there arose a sprinkling of Thoroughbred blood due principally to the aforementioned sportsmen who imported these first Thoroughbreds from England.

Quoting from "The Sportsman's Herald and Stud Book," the first American race and turf register, compiled by Patrick Nesbitt Edgar in 1831, "Until the day of Fearnought, no other than Quarter races were run in Virginia. Speed (before his importation) had been the only quality sought for; but his progeny were remarkable for their fine figures and lasting bottom; and introduced a taste (in imitation of the English) for course racing, which led the Virginians to seek for racers, horses of size and bottom, they having discovered from actual experience that strength and good wind were the most valuable and desirable qualities, and that long races were the only test of these. He may be truly said to be the Godolphin Arabian of America. He was one among the few of the first founders of Virginia horses. He was imported by the late Col. John Baylor and brought into that state in March, 1764."

While these horses were developing east of the Mississippi, unknown numbers of wild horses were roaming our Western plains. Most authorities are agreed that the origin of these Western herds was the few original horses and mares, Arabs, Barbs, and Turks, turned loose by or escaped from early Spanish explorers and settlers. Regardless of the accuracy of this origin, which personally I have reason to question, these horses had their influence on the Western horse that is today appearing.

Thus it is seen that the Western horse draws his parentage from many sources; first, the herds of wild horses or mustangs just mentioned; then the horses that carried or hauled the early settlers and traders from east to west; the strictly harness type horse from the Middle West; and the Quarter Horse, having lost favor in the Southern colonies, found his way into Tennessee, Missouri, Arkansas, the Indian Territory and the great Southwest. Also, what information I have been able to gather indicates that at the close of the Civil War many Confederate veterans forsook the tender mercies of a Yankee Congress for the law

"West of the Pecos" and took with them much of the good Thoroughbred blood of the South, which had not only given the Southern cavalry an advantage over their Northern adversaries, but as well helped to shape the horses in the land of their adoption. Such as I have enumerated are a few of the channels of inheritance that gave us our Western horses of today.

The *remudas* of a large percentage of our Western ranches even today represent a most heterogeneous lot. Occasionally a neck coming out too low between the front legs is indicative of Mexican or old Spanish influence. In many, the heavy jowls, the short, upright shoulders and low withers, coupled with powerfully-muscled loin and croup supported on calf knees, give unmistakable evidence of Quarter Horse blood. There are three general types of Quarter Horses differing somewhat in outline and general characteristics. There are the Rondos, the Billys and the Steel Dusts. What many Westerners consider a good Quarter Horse type is not a true specimen of the breed. Nine times out of ten he is a cross between a Quarter Horse and the Thoroughbred and an individual that happens to possess in large measure the good qualities of both breeds. In others the large square croups and heavy shoulders joined together by a pony body and supported on hairy legs and flat feet show that the ranch had been discovered by some Percheron stallion.

Thus to speak or to write of the Western type as if there were such a fixed type is inaccurate. The best interests of all concerned can probably be best served by admitting frankly the whole truth. For a horseman with any considerable experience in the West knows that almost no country will present a greater lack of uniformity in its horses than does our range country extending from Canada to Mexico. In this section our horses run the entire length of the scale from some of the best in the world to great herds that are fit for nothing on earth but the canning plants and the glue factories, whither thousands of them have found their way in the last few years.

From this varied background, mingling together in the hardy environment of the range country, were drawn the bands of native Western brood mares which the Remount Service at the beginning of its efforts found for its Thoroughbred sires. From the beginning of these efforts Remount officers discovered that while many ranchmen were looking for better stallions they did not know quite what they needed. To cite an instance, when I was first placed in charge of the Southern Remount Zone, a great majority of the applications for Government sires expressed a preference for Morgans, Arabs, Quarter Horses, Hambletonians, etc. But by the time I left there, four years later, by actual count ninety-eight per cent of the applications were for registered Thoroughbreds.

This change was not brought about by the Remount Service alone, but as well by the great revival of equestrian sports, principally polo, following the war, which sent hundreds of buyers scouring the ranch country in search of prospects for their trade. From these buyers, the breeders are learning that the Thoroughbred is the only sire whose get are in demand, for a far higher percentage of them possess the requisite speed, stamina and action, coupled with type or conformation that holds the saddle in place and assures balance.

Very few, if any, of the get of Arabs, Morgans, Standard-bred and Saddle-bred sires have reached this market. A knowing buyer will not drive two miles out of his way to look at a herd of these off-bred horses, because experience has taught him what to expect. The Arabs will have a carriage too high, shoulders upright and short, withers deficient with a tendency to bad hocks and lacking in speed. The Morgans, rather full and compactly made, are at first deceptive. On closer examination they are found definitely to lack galloping type. Their necks, if of sufficient length, will be too round and cresty, shoulders round with too much width between the forelegs; round barrels and short round croups; their legs, although of sturdy appearance, will lack that nicety of proportion, that placing and attachment of tendons so characteristic of the galloper. The Morgan horse, regardless of his origin, was developed in the Northern and Middle Western states and consequently for many generations was bred for, and used in harness. As a general purpose horse he was suited admirably to the needs of the farmer before the advent of the motor.

The Standard bred was clearly and definitely bred for a light harness horse. He is a trotter or pacer and not a galloper. His back is not a saddle back and his action is anything but what is wanted on a polo field, for it is high and floundering at the gallop. To ask of him any degree of collection is to throw him into a mixture of gaits that should arouse the envy of an aboriginal snake dancer. As a sire of polo prospects, I just would not mention the so-called Saddle Horse at all.

Unquestionably the most important factor bearing on the improvement of the American horse has been racing. The trotting and pacing races improved our breeds of light harness horse. The running races have had their full effect in giving us what few good riding horses we have today. The race track in the final analysis is nothing but a proving ground to test the speed, the stamina, the soundness and the temperament of sires and dams used in a general upbreeding of the American horse since the times of those earliest importations. It is equally true that many engaged in the breeding and racing of Thoroughbreds have lost sight of this original purpose and their methods have cast a shadow over the whole industry.

To witness the stupid brutality that takes place at the starting post on too many of our fairly important tracks is to send one away with disgust. I understand that this is being corrected at some of the more important tracks. But regardless of the evils attending racing, the horse users of America are indebted to it to a far greater degree than they ever suspect. The criticisms that I have levelled against racing apply to flat racing, where many seem to have forgotten that the horse is an animal and not merely a racing machine on which to place a wager. We may be thankful that in recent years brush and timber racing is gaining in popularity, especially among those who race for sport rather than profit, carrying on the tradition of colonial times.

There is a saying "history repeats itself," and the story of horse racing seems to corroborate this theory. Thirty years ago racing in our Western country was exactly where it was in the Eastern and Southern colonies just prior to the Revolutionary War. That is, the "short-horse" held a dominant position. There were but few tracks of any importance (I refer to the range section of the West and not to the Pacific Coast) and nearly all the races were match races, the distance being rarely in excess of a quarter of a mile. But in the past decade the Thoroughbred or the long distance racer is rapidly replacing the "short-horse" in popular favor there, as he did in Virginia after the importation of Fearnaught. The Thoroughbred can outrun the "short-horse" from the length of a corn cob until they both starve to death.

The growth and development of brush racing in the West is convincing increasing numbers of Westerners of the superiority of the Thoroughbred over the "short-horse." Nevertheless, there are many fortunate instances in which a careful crossing of "short-horses" with Thoroughbreds has produced most excellent results. I have in mind horses with just a touch of Quarter blood that seem to have the better qualities of both breeds. That is an individual in which the only influence of the Quarter Horse has been to add fullness and a bit of his strength and ruggedness to the general outline of a Thoroughbred.

In a former paragraph I denied the existence of a definite Western type, yet it is remarkable that horses differing as much in appearance and in breeding as do our range horses should have so many characteristics in common. Perhaps this is not so remarkable after all when we consider that every living organism is a product of two great factors—heredity and environment. Just which is the greater of these two I am not sure, but from a limited observation, I believe that in a short space of time heredity is the more important; but that in a period covering many generations environment triumphs eventually.

Inured to hardships and his semi-arid surroundings, the Western horse has his instinct of self-preservation more highly developed. He is likely to be more active, more sure of foot, and as he has been accustomed to hardships since he was a foal, he can cover longer distances; can endure greater intervals of time without food and water than can his Eastern or farm-raised brother. This is not to advocate, however, that ranchmen attempt to breed and raise good horses without grass and water. Too many such attempts have already been made.

Due to the agricultural development of the Middle West it is no longer economically possible to raise polo prospects east of the Mississippi River. This, coupled with the further fact that horses are needed to work the cattle and sheep ranches of the West, makes the range country our natural source of supply for polo prospects. Also, proper riding in "cow work" fits a pony rapidly for use as a polo pony. As a matter of fact, many of these ponies with but little stick and ball training have taken their places in good polo matches and acquitted themselves well.

In this range country are to be found many bands of excellent brood mares, and the Remount Service, as pointed out, has for the past decade or so been placing some excellent Thoroughbred sires with them. But there nevertheless exists a dearth of good brood mares throughout the range country. Also, my travels in the Eastern states have convinced me that scattered through these states is a very appreciable number of Thoroughbred mares, not wanted by Eastern breeders, that would be a great boon to our ranch breeding.

Consequently, I wonder if some plan could not be worked out between the Jockey Club, the United States Polo Association and the American Remount Service whereby these mares could be distributed among Western breeders at prices they could afford to pay. The obvious reply to this is, "Let the Western breeder come East and purchase his own mare." But those to whom this thought occurs probably do not know that ranchmen cannot borrow one dollar on horses from their bankers. This apparently is a tradition among Western bankers coming down from the days when horses were so plentiful in the West as to constitute almost a nuisance.

In writing of the American horse one must give first credit to the Blue Grass section of Kentucky and those far-seeing breeders who have given us this great Thoroughbred nursery that has sent sires and dams into every

WHITE STOCKINGS

Famous running mare recently taken to Mexico, now owned by J. D. Raines in Mexico City. She is a Louisiana bred Quarter mare and a great running horse.

LADY SPECK AND DON MANNERS

Finish of the now famous race between a Quarter mare and a clean bred Thoroughbred run at Kingsville, Texas, last year. The time was 22-3/5 seconds for a standing start quarter, and Lady Speck, the Quarter mare, got the decision. Lady Speck next to the camera.

BROWN JUG

Brown Jug was by Jim Ned and was one of the top stallions owned by William Anson of Christoval, Texas. Jim Ned was sired by Pancho who was by Billy.

SAM JONES

Sam Jones was sired by Yellow Wolf and belonged to William Anson. He was 17 years old at the time this photograph was taken.

state in the Union. They have meant to our Western breeders what England meant to the early colonists.

"It is an ill wind that blows no good," and oddly enough a few of our great strains of Western horses owe their origin today to outlaws who bred them with a hope of outdistancing sheriff's posses and vigilante committees. I could mention several of these strains, but unfortunately they bear the names of their breeders and these breeders were so successful in producing fast horses that they lived to leave behind them a considerable and active progeny.

In one of our Western towns there lived a man of such great age that he was interviewed by an Eastern writer. "To what do you owe your long life?" he was asked. After a moment's hesitation the old man replied, "Well, you see it's this way. At the time Bill Smith was killed I had a much faster horse than Sheriff Buck Jones had, and that probably had a lot to do with it."

"Short-Horses"
By BOB DENHARDT

"THE AMERICAN QUARTER HORSE is not only an established breed of remote origin, but he is a most useful type for nearly all Western ranch purposes." William Anson said this in 1910, and three decades later in 1940 the same is true of the Quarter Horse. In fact, today even more can be said, for now there is established the American Quarter Horse Association, which has been organized to create a studbook and registry and to promote the Quarter Horse in every way possible. The Quarter Horse is still considered by most ranchers as the ideal Western horse.

The Quarter Horse is a stock horse as well as a race horse, but there is about as much resemblance between the pure Quarter Horse and an ordinary cow horse as there is between the Arabian and an Indian pony. Besides the difference in conformation the Quarter Horse is a breed which will reproduce itself faithfully, and stamp its offspring with its own peculiarly good points—this even when crossed with what is probably the most prepotent blood in the world, that of the Thoroughbred race horse.

The ancestors of the Quarter Horse came to Texas with the first settlers, for the most part from Tennessee, Missouri, and Illinois. The Arabian horse gained his fame on the desert, the Percheron on the succulent grasses of La Perche, the Welsh on the scanty herbage of the Welsh hills, but it was in the mesquite and pear valleys and the rocky limestone hills of West Texas that the Quarter Horse rose to fame.

"I am confident that there is not a horse in England, not perhaps in the whole world, that can excel the Quarter Horses in rapid speed, and these, likewise, make excellent horses for the road." These words were written *two hundred* years ago, but the same can be said today. The words were written by an early English visitor to the American colonies before the Revolutionary War. He said the Southerners loved short races, particularly when matched between two horses for a quarter of a mile. This is still true, although the scene has shifted west across the Mississippi River and into Louisiana, Texas, Arizona, and New Mexico. In the Southwest every Sunday and holiday these short races take place. They are as native as the boots, the curl brimmed hats, and the soft drawl.

The fact that the Quarter Horse is the oldest distinct breed of American horses is not questioned by those who have studied history, but this fact frequently surprises those less informed. Writers before the Revolutionary War and before the establishment of the Thoroughbred definitely stated that there was in America a breed of short distance running horses called Quarter Horses. The American Studbook of the Thoroughbred horse recognized the existence of the Quarter Horse before they were established. They admit that certain of their foundation animals were Quarter Horses.

In the second volume of the American Studbook there is a list of stallions whose ancestry was necessary to tabulate the foundation of pedigrees for Bruce's Studbook. Among these we find listed, "Cherokee, Quarter Horse." He sired stallions whose blood still runs in many American Thoroughbred families. In Edgar's Studbook, which Bruce used as a foundation for the present studbook of the Thoroughbred, we find many horses entered just as Quarter Horses. Hamilton Busby, one of the best authorities on Thoroughbred pedigrees, told William Anson that the Quarter Horse entered into the pedigrees of American Thoroughbreds in a large way—particularly those originating in Illinois. This latter has been true up to modern times.

Illinois has been the home of one of the greatest Quarter Horse families, the Dan Tucker-Peter McCue line. The only other families that compare at all are the Steel Dusts and the Rondos. In 1888 Samuel Watkins of Petersburg, Illinois, owned and raced many Quarter Horses, but chief among these were Barney Owens and Joe Sefus. Joe could run the quarter in the very low time of $22\frac{1}{2}$ seconds. Breeding these horses, he raised Dan Tucker, which he also raced until he eventually sold him to Thomas Trammell of Sweetwater, Texas. Watkins bred Dan Tucker before he sold him and got a horse he called Hi Henry. Mr. Watkins raced Hi Henry also with great success. Hi Henry still holds the Lake Side track record at five-eighths of a mile which he ran in under a minute. Joe Sefus and Barney Owens were the basis for all of the fast horses in central Illinois. Trammell liked Dan Tucker so well he went back to Illinois and bought Barney Owens. When Dan Tucker and Barney Owens were taken to Texas they sired almost all of the Trammell and Newman racers, including such famous horses as Pan Zareta, Don Domo, Dora Woods, and May Beach. Peter McCue, raised by Watkins, also goes to Dan Tucker. He sired Money Muss, Agnes Mae, Turns Tricks (who held the world's five-eighths mile record until it was broken by his cousin, Pan Zareta). Never Fret, Buck Thomas, Harry D. (who won seventeen races in one winter at Tia Juana), and many others. Today the Dan Tucker-Peter McCue blood is found in a majority of American Quarter Horses. This blood was carried by such descendants as Harmon Baker, Hickory Bill, Joe

Hancock, Buck Thomas, Little Joe (New Mexico), Rainy Day, Midnight, Jack McCue, and many others.

Much of the superior soundness and constitution of the American Thoroughbred over his Continental brothers is undoubtedly due to the infusion of Quarter Horse blood. Maybe here, too, lies the secret of his great success in the shorter distance, say six and seven furlongs up to and including a mile. American Thoroughbreds are better sprinters than they are stayers, and in the same vein, most of the outstanding records made by American horses have been made in the short distance events. Quarter Horse blood may not have helped the American Thoroughbred in long distance racing, but it certainly has not detracted from his value in many other ways.

Old Sam Harper was one of the best mile horses of his day, and his dam was a Quarter Horse mare. Pan Zareta held the record for the five-eighths mile, and many claim her sire was a Quarter Horse. Take the famous old race horse Charlie Wilson. Charlie was raised by John Nasworthy of San Angelo around 1889. Racing under his breeder's colors he was, as far as is known, never beaten up to three-quarters of a mile. Sold later, he was taken to Chicago and there became involved in a scandal and was ruled off the turf, but he won the races as he pleased at Guttenberg and other outlaw tracks. He was sired by the Thoroughbred Buck Walton, and his dam was out of a mare of Quarter Horse breeding.

Arch Oldham, famous race horse of one of the greatest of Texas Quarter Horse breeders, Crawford Sykes, was bred along the same lines. Arch was sired by imported Gallantry, but out of a Quarter mare. He was registered for racing purposes only. Sykes bred him in the spring and summer and raced with great success in the fall and winter. Crawford Sykes used Arch Oldham as a sire on his Rondo mares, and produced some of the best Quarter Horses to come out of Southwest Texas. Crawford Sykes also purchased Whalebone from Billy Blanton when Billy had had a string of bad luck. What with Rondo, Whalebone, Arch Oldham, and his other great horses, it is small wonder Sykes of Karnes County, Texas, is recalled as the greatest early breeder of South Texas.

Since there has not been, until the last year, a studbook for Quarter Horses, they have been bred more for type and performance than from blood lines and pedigrees. Although few Quarter Horses can lay claim to pure lineage, almost without exception they show the conformation characteristics which have been so firmly established. Regardless of what breed is mated to the Quarter Horse, he will transmit unmistakable racial characteristics to his offspring. Among the usual characteristics of the Quarter Horse are a strong back and loin, immense musculature, especially in the forearm and gaskins, a great weight per hand, good feet, and sturdy legs.

Billy Anson once said regarding the Quarter Horse: It is a horse " . . . which will fill the want of the Western rancher, or any man who wishes to breed an animal which will be equally useful as a cow horse, buggy horse, and if necessary, farm horse; a horse which is appreciated when taken to New York or other Eastern points, whether used for riding, driving, or for the game of polo." William Anson knew, because he raised them, took them East, played polo on them, and sold them to the Army.

The Quarter Horse is today generally recognized as one of the best and most widely used of the Western horses.

The Quarter Horse, A History
By BOB DENHARDT

IN THE NINETEENTH CENTURY Texas had a horse of which it was justifiably proud, because its equal in working cattle had never been bred. Coming first with that bow-legged stockman, Cortés, the horse had followed the Spanish cattle ever northward until it found what was a heaven for horses in the plains of Texas. For 350 years these horses had been working with cattle, and when they reached Texas they were a race of animals capable of unbelievable feats of endurance and endowed with a cow sense seemingly inbred in the race.

The Texans, typical horsemen, would bet their last shirt on the prowess of their horses, and the stage was all set for the appearance of Steel Dust, one of the best Quarter Horses ever bred. The stories of his arrival are so numerous and varied that one can only take the similar features and weave from these an outline of the true story. It seems someone in Texas had a horse he was mighty proud of and his fame spread as he defeated all comers. Many of the reports give his name as Shilo, while others say Shilo was another Quarter Horse which had come into Texas. Anyway, at this time, Steel Dust arrived. It is possible that someone had brought him with the express purpose of defeating the Texas horse, but what is more likely is that his owner was just on the move. We do know that sometime in the early 1800's Steel Dust was matched with a champion Texas horse. Steel Dust's quiet demeanor disarmed the natives and the thorough defeat of the Texas horse very nearly bankrupted the community. From then on the Quarter Horse was made. Every Texan who had a good mare wanted to breed her to a Quarter Horse stallion.

The blood of the Eastern Quarter Horse mingled with the Texas blood, and all of his urge to work with cattle came out in this new cross. The Quarter Horse and his get created a marked improvement in the conformation of the Texas cow horse, without detracting from his cow sense and stamina. The result was the best cow horse the Southwest had known. Now the cow horse of Texas had added weight and a fresh burst of speed without any loss of that intuitive cow sense which the centuries had bred in the Spanish horse. To this date Quarter Horses, or Steel Dusts, as they are often called, are the best stock horses in the world.

The Quarter Horse has distinct characteristics, and horsemen can tell offsprings bearing a half or a quarter blood. Prepotency is one of the surest signs of long breeding. As types are not fixed in a few generations, it is not surprising to find a long line of ancestors possessing like qualities behind the Quarter Horse. Typical Quarter Horse characteristics are small, alert ears, a well-developed neck, sloping shoulders, short deep barrel, a great heart girth, heavy muscled in thigh and forearm, legs not too long, and firmly jointed with the knee and pastern close. All of these features but accentuate his peculiar abilities. Rarely does the Quarter Horse exceed 15 hands, but due to his build will often reach 1,200 pounds or more. It is this fact which led Dan Casement, one of the best of present day authorities, to say that here is more horse for the height than is found in any other breed.

Much of the origin of the Quarter Horse is lost, but a few facts are available. Wood, Sandys, and Gookin were the first to import English horses into Virginia about 1620. Soon thereafter, Governor Nicholson legalized horse racing, which had immediately become popular. By 1690 large purses were being offered. For several reasons, among these the lack of tracks and straight stretches of road, it became the habit to run short races, generally along the main street of the town, which was the only straight and cleared stretch available. J. F. D. Smith, who made a tour of the colonies prior to the Revolutionary War, said that the colonists were very much attached to quarter racing, which was generally a match between two horses running a quarter of a mile. He said that the colonists had a breed of horses (Quarter Horses) which performed it with astounding velocity. Horse racing was also popular in Rhode Island. William Robinson, one-time Deputy Governor of Rhode Island, raised some of the best running horses in that colony. His original sire, Old Snipe, according to an unsigned manuscript, was found in a drove of wild horses on Point Judith. Although Robinson did not realize it, Old Snipe's ancestors were Arabians, probably bred in Andalusia or Cordoba in Spain. It was not long until Robinson horses were famous for their speed. An intercolonial match was arranged between the horses of Virginia and Rhode Island. So successful were the Spanish horses from Rhode Island that the Virginians obtained some of Old Snipe's progeny to improve their horses. Now the Spanish blood was being crossed with imported English blood. The Quarter Horse was arriving.

Very likely the Virginia horses already had some infusion of Spanish blood, as it is known that there were Spanish horses in the backwoods of the colony. This point is borne out further by a description of the Virginia horse at this time. Hugh Jones in 1724 described them as "not very tall but hardy, strong and fleet." The wild Spanish horses did not come from De Soto's expeditions as had been commonly supposed, but from the Spanish settlement of Guale. This district, composed of the southeastern section of the present United States, had by 1650 seventy-nine missions, eight large towns, and many ranches, some supported by the Crown. The constant raids of the English and the Indians on the Guale settlements spread Spanish livestock far into the North. Soon most of the southern English colonies had wild horses in the backwoods. Capturing wild horses was a favorite sport among the young colonials, especially in Virginia and Carolina. Wild cattle were also captured in "cowpens" by the colonial "cowboys," already so-called in the seventeenth century, riding their fast Quarter Horses. A famous Revolutionary War battle was fought at one of these cowpens.

The colonial short distance horse was established in the American colonies at a date too early to allow the English Thoroughbred to have much influence on his breeding, and later, when he was raced against them, he could beat them on short distances due to his marvelous start. It must have been disconcerting to these English Thoroughbred owners to import their running horses, those greyhounds of English turfs, and have them left at the post by the short but thick-set and close-coupled animal of the colonies. Janus is apparently the only horse imported at this time whose blood influenced the "Quarter-of-a-Mile" running horse. Anson, one of the earliest stockmen to interest himself in the history of the Quarter Horse, says, "From all accounts and the number of Januses which appear in all pedigrees, he must have been as prolific as our own Texas Steel Dust, undoubtedly the most prolific horse which ever stood on four legs."

In Patrick Nisbett Edgar's Studbook *(The American Race-Turf Register,* N. Y., 1833) we find in the preface that in the early days quarter racing was much in fashion. Listed in this volume are many horses with the following abbreviations after them: C. A. Q. R. H. (Celebrated American Quarter Running Horse); F. A. Q. R. H. (Famous American Quarter Running Horse); or C. A. Q. R. M. (Celebrated American Quarter Running Mare). It is rather interesting to read some of these entries:

"Old Bacchus" . . . F. A. Q. R. H. . . . very heavily made for his height, 14.2 hands, foaled 1774, gotten by C. A. Q. R. H. "Old Babram." Died 1789.

"Little Bacchus" . . . 14 hands . . . sired by "Old Bacchus," foaled 1778.

"Red Bacchus" . . . C. A. Q. R. H. . . . Bay, 14.1 hands, heavily muscled.

"Dash" . . . C. A. Q. R. M. . . . She was one of the swiftest Quarter nags in the world of her day and won a vast deal of money.

People who feel that the Quarter Horse is just an offshoot of the American Thoroughbred should read with interest the dates on these entries and see that the Thoroughbred was founded with the help of the Quarter Horse. One of the facts which demonstrates this is that a large number of horses and mares in the first two volumes of Sanders D. Bruce's Studbook (*The American Studbook,* N. Y., 1873) are described as Quarter Horses in Edgar's Studbook. When they were transcribed by Bruce from Edgar's book into his own book, this fact was left out.

It is even possible that Justin Morgan was a Quarter Horse. William Anson said that this was generally admitted, adding that Stillman and members of the Morgan Horse Club of New York admitted he could have been nothing else. Major Grove Cullum, an authority on Western horses, who until a few years ago was head horse buyer for the Remount Service and is now with the New Mexico Racing Commission, feels that, inasmuch as Quarter racing was popular in colonial times, it is possible that Justin Morgan was a Quarter Horse.

Steel Dust is the most famous of all Quarter Horses, although much of the detail of his life is lost in the maze of legends which surround him. As one ranchman put it, Steel Dust would turn over in his grave if he knew how many "broomtails" were sold under his name. Every horse trader who has not recently joined a church will modestly admit that his horses are direct descendants of Steel Dust. Wherever cattle are handled in the open and rodeos promoted by stockmen, Quarter Horse blood can be seen, whether they are called Steel Dusts, Billy Horses, Printers, Copper-Bottoms, Kentucky Whips, Cold Decks, Rondos, or any of the various names inherited from some famous Quarter Horse sire.

We have few reliable descriptions of Steel Dust, Billy, Shilo, and other of the principal founders of the Quarter Horse strain in Texas, but the startling uniformity of their descendants gives us a rather clear picture of their appearance. Steel Dust animals can be told from any other Quarter Horse just as readily as a Quarter Horse can be told from other breeds. Another important Quarter Horse family which exists today is the Billy Horse. To the casual observer, the Billy might more closely resemble a compact Thoroughbred than would a Steel Dust. This is due to the infusion of Thoroughbred blood between 1890 and 1915 by racing men. Billy Horses, however, do not resemble Thoroughbreds. Doubtless, devotees of both breeds would object to such a statement. Steel Dusts are shorter in the neck and shoulders, more compact and closer to the ground than either the Billy or the Thoroughbred. The forearm and the rear quarters of the Thoroughbred are not so heavily muscled. Seemingly, the Quarter Horse has more muscle on the outside and inside of the leg and hindquarters, while the Thoroughbred is muscled principally on the inside. Steel Dusts have the smooth and compact shape, short back and deep barrel of the Quarter Horse, but the unusually heavy musculature which stamps the breed seems to reach in the Steel Dust a peak which "amounts to almost a deformity in his bulging jaw." This also explains why the Steel Dust strain is occasionally referred to as "Big Jaws." Anson termed it a "coarseness of the head." Dan Casement says, "These massive jaws seem to serve as a fitting symbol of the tenacity and determination which mark the Steel Dust strain. They make a strange contrast to the alert little ears that denote the keenness of the horse's sensibilities, and furnish a substantial background for the forehead and eyes that bespeak deep stores of equine wisdom." Those who are acquainted with the Criollo Horse of the Argentine will see a striking resemblance in the general conformation of the two animals.

Steel Dusts and Billy were undoubtedly the first Quarter Horses to make a marked impression on the cow horses of the West. Other strains of the Quarter Horses as well as different members of the Steel Dust family have established branches of the Quarter Horse family in the Southwest. Some of the better known are the Steel Dusts and Billy horses mentioned above, Cold Decks, Printers, Rondos, Copper-Bottoms, and the Blake horse. All are offshoots of the main Quarter Horse family. The Blake horse is of the Cold Deck (see illustration facing page 199) line of Steel Dusts and was developed by S. C. Blake of Pryor, Oklahoma. Major Cullum of the Remount Service has stated they are the best Quarter Horses he has ever seen. In 1921 Mr. Blake presented the Remount Service with a Quarter Horse called Tramp. Tramp, an excellent Quarter Horse, was by Tubal-Cain by Cold Deck by old Cold Deck by Steel Dust. The dam of Tubal-Cain was by Alsup's Red Buck.

Copper-Bottoms were found mostly in Central West Texas. Copper-Bottoms normally weighed about 100 pounds less than the other Quarter Horses, but with their splendid withers and fine pasterns and refined heads were among the most aristocratic of all Quarter Horses. R. L. Underwood of Wichita Falls has one of the last pureblood Copper-Bottoms in his Golden Chief (see illustration facing page 86). Mr. Underwood's horse, Dexter, is a son of the Copper-Bottom stallion Chief and a Steel Dust mare; and, although he resembles his sire more than his dam, he combines many of the best features of the two.

Rondo horses are offshoots of the Billy horses. The original Billy horse came to Texas from Kentucky in 1865 and was brought in by Bill Fleming. There is strong evidence that he was a son of Steel Dust. Billy sired many great stallions, such as Red Rover, Jim Brown, Midnight, and McCoy Billy. The last horse sired Rondo. Rondo, who was owned by Crawford Sykes, produced many great horses, such as Big Jim, Old Mae, Little Joe II, Baby Ruth, Nettie Harrison, Kitty, Blue Eye, and Old Jenny. Peter McCue (see illustration facing page 70) was bred up in Petersburg, Illinois, by the famous Watkins family, which produced such great short distance horses as Dan Tucker, Barney Owens, and Hi Henry. Peter McCue was the sire of Harmon Baker (see illustration facing page 86), Hickory Bill, Buck Thomas, John Wilkins, Turns Tricks, Money Muss, Never Fret, Coal Oil Johnnie, Kitty McCue, Midnight, and many other notable horses.

One of the earliest stockmen to become well known as a breeder of Quarter Horses was William Anson of Cristoval, Texas. Billy Anson came from an aristocratic English family, and, like so many of the younger sons of the English nobility, came to the New World during the last half of the nineteenth century to seek his fortune. It is said that, although he became a real Westerner in the best sense of the word, he never lost his accent or English manner.

Anson got his best opportunity to collect Quarter Horses when he was buying horses for the British government during the Boer War. While gathering large numbers of horses he was able to obtain for himself a number of excellent Quarter Horses, particularly of the Steel Dust stamp. With these as a base, he began to breed them on his Head-of-the-River Ranch on the Concho. He crossed several of the blood lines, buying Harmon Baker, a son of Peter McCue, and an Arch Oldham horse from Crawford

Sykes. Perhaps the outstanding stud which he produced was Jim Ned. Jim Ned sired two very famous colts. One was Brown Jug (see illustration facing page 135), who went to Mexico. Concho Colonel was the other well-known son of Jim Ned, and he was bought and bred by Dan Casement. With Concho Colonel, Casement bred Balleymooney (see illustration facing page 6), who in turn sired such well-known modern horses as Red Dog (see illustration facing page 6), Frosty, Billy Byrne, and Deuce, all of whom are bearing the well-known Casement Triangle-Bar brand. Anson wrote several articles on the breed, being one of the first men to study the history of the Quarter Horse, and blood of his horses is found in many of the best Quarter Horse studs in the country. In many ways Dan D. Casement has taken Mr. Anson's place as the foremost breeder and authority.

At about the same time there were two other centers in Texas, around Alice and Sweetwater, where breeders were developing some great Quarter Horses. Both used Peter McCue blood from the Watkins line in Illinois.

Thus, we have the Quarter Horse arising in the English colonies with much of his blood coming from Spain. In the short races, which ranged from ten or thirty yards up to a furlong or a quarter, certain characteristics were developed. Outstanding among these were his cool head, compact body, and muscles of spring steel, capable of split-second speed. Endurance and hardness he got from his Spanish dams, and his speed and grace from infusions of occasional Thoroughbred blood which happened to match his small size, compact build, and sturdy muscles. There is an old saying that Quarter Horses can run as far and as fast as they can hold their breath. Whether this is true or not is questionable, but anyone who has tried to get an extra ounce of energy for some action can understand it.

As the new American nation moved ever westward, the Quarter Horse and his owner were always in the lead, each new country providing new races and new admirers of the breed.

The Southwestern Cow-Horse
By BOB DENHARDT

THE "GREAT AMERICAN DESERT" was relegated to the Indians by Monroe, considered in the days of Jackson as a fortunate barrier prohibiting Americans from straggling across the country, and repeatedly characterized by such men as Catlan as being then and forever useless to cultivating man. Then, suddenly, undaunted into the "Great Plains" came the cow-horse, leading and flanking vast herds of cattle, viciously snapping at any animal which dared stray from line. From the immense stretches of Texas and New Mexico the southwestern cow-horse pushed the cattle northward into the land of the Indian nations and toward a railroad which was pushing into the waste. Farther and farther the cattle went, searching for markets and pastures, until finally they had spread from Matamoros to Manitoba. It was the cow-horse which ended the reign of the Great American Desert, making the land his own. In search for grass he crossed every divide, rode into every coulee, swam every stream. A land was found which could breed wealth, cattle companies springing up like mushrooms after a rain until no vocation could compare with the calling of the cow-horse in its halcyon days during the last third of the nineteenth century.

Settlers, cheap barbed wire, the difficulty of segregating "customary ranges" on crowded land, these and other factors finally led to fencing. Fewer cow-horses were needed in fenced pastures and improved breeding was possible. In place of the ubiquitous "longhorn," a white-faced Hereford appeared. Although the cattle ranch of the old days and its picturesque life were gone, the cowboys and the cow-horse were still present and the cattle baron was still the nabob of the American uplands. Stock-horses were just as necessary in the handling of cattle as ever before.

The drive of the Texas men has become a saga. Picture gaunt, dust-caked, nervous longhorns coming over a rise in the prairie with dilated nostrils eagerly twitching for the smell of water. A long black line disappearing into a trail of dust. Will James caught some of the elemental restlessness of this scene in his "Trail Herd." Nor did he forget to put into the picture the ever-present, all-important cow-horse. The long drives carried the cow-horse of the Southwest to wherever range cattle are found. Four hundred years of heritage had at last blossomed. The heyday of the cow-horse occurred during the decades between

1866 and 1885. Without him and the "longhorn," part of America could never have been built. The latter part of this same period saw this same cow-horse changed in some localities almost beyond recognition. His blood was being diluted by driving-, draft-, and running-horses brought in by the Easterners, a people to whom "appearance" and "value" were almost synonymous. It was too much to expect a people used to tall, slender running horses or heavy draft horses to believe that an animal not much larger than a stocky pony could have the intelligence, stamina, and endurance to outwork on the cattle range half a dozen of their animals. All this entirely neglected one little feature called "cow-sense" which the Eastern horses coming from northern Europe seemingly lacked.

In the mountain ranges of the Northwest the new cattle owners thought there was a demand for large horses to carry weight in the rough country, but with each gain they made in weight there was a corresponding drop in endurance and cow-sense. In Oregon Clydesdale sires were used in a few cases, it must be admitted with fair success, but they were commonly called the "Oregon Lummox," no doubt most apt for the majority. In Montana and the Dakotas, Percherons were used with identical results, and alongside of the agile cow-horse doubtless deserved their appellation, "Percheron Puddin'-Foots."

In California, led by the famous Miller-Lux outfit which boasted they could drive from Canada to Mexico and camp every night on their own land, the mustang was crossed with Morgan blood and again a larger horse was produced. Many of these animals became good cowhorses. Dutch economy had found a way to have a plow horse after age had slowed down needed agility. Most polo ponies are today bred by using Thoroughbred stallions and cow-horse dams, the product being as good a polo horse as the breeders are likely to beget. But then, as Graham says, "Polo players ride for pleasure and their horses are fed and pampered like Christians."

By crossing the Thoroughbred, the Morgan, the Clydesdale and the Percheron, with the lowly cow-horse, a taller and heavier horse was produced, one that could run faster, or one more fitted for the parade, or the plow. But, strange though it may seem, these are not the only things for which horses are bred. The cross was larger, faster and stronger, but soft and unfit to work with cattle. When the cowman had to travel over rough country with perhaps no food or water all day, then, work over, follow a bunch of steers home under the stars, or sleep in the open on an icy night, or with a scorching wind drying out the grass, it began to dawn on him that his new half-breed was not equal to such work. Besides being clumsy on the turn, slow off the mark, and unsafe for running in rough country, he was an inferior weight carrier. A cold night or two without his blanket and his grain made a poor horse of him.

While the breeding in the northern rim of the cow country was for weight, in the Southwest a new factor entered the picture which was for the first time to improve on the Spanish cow-horse. It all started some time soon after the Civil War. The Texans lost a race and the Southwestern horsemen had a new ideal; his name was Steel Dust. Steel Dust was a Quarter Horse, but so prepotent that even today horses bearing his blood can be recognized by experts. As for his family, the Quarter Horse, even the unitiated may recognize his features with but a little practice. Small, alert ears; sloping shoulders; short, deep barrel; extremely heavy musculature of thigh and forearm, particularly on the outside of the latter; legs not very long but firmly jointed; knee and pastern close: all of these are his characteristics. Rarely does the Quarter Horse exceed fourteen hands, but, because of his build, weights of well over 1,000 are not unusual.

To people unacquainted with the history of the real American horse, and there are few references to him, even in college textbooks, the origin of the Quarter Horse is an enigma. It is not until the extensive mission and ranch system of the Spanish Florida in the 1600's is studied; it is not until it is realized that the word "cowboy" was already in use in Virginia and Maryland in the seventeenth century; it is not until the full significance of the word "cowpens" in a Revolutionary War battle by that name is grasped; that the origin of the Quarter Horse is a complete story.

It was in Spanish Guale, from which Florida and Georgia were later carved, that horses and cattle got their start on the Atlantic seaboard. The English arrived late in the New World, but with their customary vigor were soon raiding the Spanish settlements of Guale looking for horses and cattle. With the help of the Indians, they succeeded. Where there are men who love horses, there are horse races (except in those few places where certain groups legislate against temptation), and so here in the early colonies the men matched their horses as all men have since Biblical times. The lack of cleared spaces, tracks, and facilities proved no detriment. They raced their horses down the main street of the town—a distance seldom exceeding a quarter of a mile. They became known then as Quarter Horses, since they were bred and trained to run distances up to a quarter of a mile. After the Civil War many of the Southerners moved west and the Quarter Horse began to arrive in the Southwest in numbers great enough to influence the old Spanish cow-horse.

This new horse, produced by the cross of the Spanish cow-horse and the Quarter Horse, had all the features which the rancher of the Southwest valued most in saddle animals. They could run and work. Quarter Horses had been selectively bred for generations to produce a horse which would fairly fly over short distances, as many English Thoroughbred owners have discovered to their everlasting regret. The cow-horse, on the other hand, had been bred by the merciless law of the survival of the fittest until his endurance and stamina were unequalled. Both traced their ancestors to the Spanish Arab and the Barb blood. The cross of the Spanish cow-horse and the Quarter Horse improved both animals. The cow-horse got a bit more weight, a new burst of speed, and some of his hard angles smoothed out. The Quarter Horse's recessive trait to handle cattle was renewed and the ability to travel day after day on meager natural grass was implanted. The good points of both horses were brought out to a superlative degree by this cross. Now a horse considered by many cattlemen as the greatest cow-horse ever developed had arrived. Speed to overtake the fastest calf, weight to hold the heaviest steer, endurance to work day after day, and finally a desire and love to work with cattle.

Today the popularity of the Quarter Horse is rapidly spreading with breeders located from Kansas to California and from Utah to Louisiana. One large breeder has purchased some three hundred Quarter-type mares for breeding purposes during the last three years. Whether they are called Steel Dusts, Copper-Bottoms, Cold Decks, Billys, Rondos, Printers, or any other name, they all belong to the Quarter Horse family. There is today a growing sentiment to establish a Studbook and Registry for these horses, and doubtless some time in the near future such an organization will arise. A Steel Dust breeder in Colorado recently wrote an article in the *Denver Record Stockman* advocating just such an organization; two other articles appeared in current issues of the *Western Horseman* compiling much of the available data concerning the Quarter Horse; and at the last Fort Worth Livestock Show a small group of Quarter Horse enthusiasts got together for a dinner to discuss Quarter Horses and to consider the possibilities of an organization. All indications point to the early recognition of this wonder horse of the southwestern range.

It is indeed unfortunate that a breed of horses, as useful and popular as the western horse, has never received sufficient recognition. The principal reason for this in the past has been the lack of sufficient interest by the ranchers of the West. They have continued using and breeding their horses but have not cared to publicize or cooperate. Today we have the odd situation where the most popular horse in the country has no official recognition and yet he has every right to that recognition. In our agricultural college textbooks, presuming to teach types and market classes of livestock, sections are devoted to the American Saddle Horse, the Standard-bred, and the Morgan. Yet no section is devoted to the western stockhorse, who has been used longer, is more numerous, is ridden by more people, and has been more useful than perhaps all the others put together.

The Colonial Quarter Horse
By J. GOODWIN HALL

THE QUARTER HORSE of the olden times owes his early and prominent existence to the Colonial Cavaliers, the masters of Virginia and of the Carolinas, who were the first men in America to begin the breeding of horses for purposes of racing and for their general improvement.

Quarter racing in the colony and State of Virginia was the most popular sport of the Cavalier colonists. These immigrants to Virginia brought with them, and their descendants retained, all the love for the horse and for racing. Military training had brought them the advantage of being well mounted.

Horse breeding began in Virginia upon a foundation stock of "17 horses and mares" brought over from England by Sir Thomas Dale in 1611, and "20 mares" sent out by the Virginia Company in 1620. These importations were average saddle horses bred in England before the general dissemination of Arabian blood; they were characteristically cold blooded. Horses increased in number rapidly after their introduction, and the records show that by 1668 a native breed was firmly established; and it was about this time that Quarter racing became a popular pastime. The settlers became a race of unsurpassed riders. The ownership of a good horse was not only a necessity, but a matter of pleasure and pride.

The quarter running horse prior to 1740 was produced through crossing the native Virginia horse with Indian ponies. No evidence can be found that the Virginia Indians had horses when the colonists first made contact with them. There is ample evidence, however, that the Southern Indians, the Cherokees, Chickasaws, Choctaws, Creeks and Seminoles had domesticated horses in the 17th and 18th centuries. They were descendants of the horses brought over by the Spanish explorers.

The first horses landed in the United States were brought into Florida in 1527 by Panfilo de Narvaez, 42 in number, but these all perished or were killed.

A large force of troops mounted on Spanish horses accompanied De Soto on his explorations in which he discovered the Mississippi. Many of the horses of this exploration were lost, strayed and stolen, and they were the first importation. The survivors ranged wild, and in the course of time they, along with survivors of other Spanish explorers, greatly increased in number. In 1678 there were large bands of wild horses descended from the old Spanish horses and from wanderers of the Virginia stock roaming over the southern and western parts of America. The ponies of the southern Indians were active and hardy but small, rarely exceeding $13\frac{1}{2}$ hands in height. The mares, when crossed with the native Virginia horse, produced beautiful horses of substance and speed.

The honor of having bred, reared and developed an especial type of short distance race horse, the Quarter Horse, belongs to Virginia. At the time of the Civil War Virginia was known as the race horse region of America, and the expression, "Virginia Horse," from Maine to Florida and as far west as the Mississippi River was taken to mean a superior animal. This early American equine athlete was from the early part of the 17th century, and is down to this very day, the general utility horse of America, superior in endurance, quick burst of speed and all-around performance, docility and in good temper to any other race of general horses in the world. He was satisfactory for the plow, wagon or coach, as well as the turf, field and the road. The Quarter Horse played a gallant and prominent role in the Revolutionary War and the Civil War, and in the exploration and development of our great West.

Quarter Horses were the prominent leaders of the equine F. F. V. aristocracy several generations before the advent of distance racing and the importations of the English running horse.

The source records of the Quarter Horse and quarter racing speak of the quality of the early American horse and the fondness of the people for racing. The exact date of the first quarter race in Virginia cannot be ascertained, but we do know that the earliest record of a quarter race bears the date September 10, 1674, Enrico County, Virginia. As far back as the 12th century there were regular races in England. In the reign of James I annual races were held at several places in the Kingdom and became a favorite sport of the people. The earliest notices of "short" racing occur in English records prior to 1600.

There can be no doubt that quarter racing was practiced and became the popular sport of the Virginia colonists more than 200 years before the American Thoroughbred became a breed.

Between 1730 and the beginning of the Revolutionary War, Virginia was an exceedingly prosperous community. Tobacco and other agricultural products brought high prices, and the gentlemen who owned the old plantations along the Rappahannock and the James Rivers had ample means to import and produce for themselves as good horses as existed. Bulle Rock, foaled about 1718, was the first English race horse landed (1730) on Virginia soil. He was followed to Virginia by Dabster (1741), Crab (1746),

Monkey (1747), Jolly Roger (1748), Morton's Traveller (1750), Silver Eye (1751), Childers (1751), Booth's Janus (1757) and Fearnought (1765). These importations, crossed on native mares, improved the quarter running horse and helped produce a breed of horses which eventually became the American Thoroughbred. The source records describe this type as a horse almost identical with our present day Quarter Horse. The earlier stallions of Virginia averaged about 14½ hands in height and yet Virginia in those days had a stock of general horses equal to any in the world. Many of the earliest racers were under 14 hands in height.

In 1700 the average height of the English racer was 13 hands 3 inches. The celebrated Gimcrack (1760), is supposed to have been 13 hands, 3 inches in height.

Skinner & Mason's Farrier, published in 1857, had this to say about the early imported English stock:

> "They have produced stock of vast size, bone and substance, and at the same time endowed with such extraordinary and before unheard of powers of speed and continuance as to render it probable that individuals of them have reached nature's ultimate point of perfection."

To properly cover the history of quarter racing and the Quarter Horse would require one or more volumes of several hundred pages, and the history of the Virginia breeders and patrons of the Quarter Horse would require lengthy writing.

Some of the most distinguished breeders of Celebrated and Famous American Quarter Horses and patrons of

Quarter Racing were Colonel John Tayloe of Mount Airy, Colonel Hoomes of Bowling Green, the Randolphs (John of Roanoke and William of Cumberland), John C. Goode of Mecklenburgh, Hon. Willis Alston, North Carolina, and Wyllie Jones.

The General Studbook by Edgar (1833) contains the pedigrees of over 70 Famous and Celebrated American Quarter Running Horses and over 100 of their descendants.

The early American Quarter Horse was one of the important tap roots of the American Thoroughbred. Pedigrees of Famous and Celebrated American Quarter Horses and their descendants, more than 200, were included in Bruce's American Studbook (1868), the official record of the foundation stock of the American Thoroughbred. The following pedigrees and descriptions were taken from Edgar's Studbook. They are also listed in the American Studbook (Bruce):

BABRAM

The F. A. Q. R. H. (Old) bred by the late Mr. John Goode, Senr. of Mecklenburgh Co., Va.; foaled about the year 1766:

Got by the I. H. Old Janus—I. H. Old Janus—I. H. Jolly Roger—I. H. Silver Eye—I. H. Old Monkey.

Character: Babram was one of the very best Quarter (of a mile) Racers in America of his day. In running a quarter race with Old Jupiter over Lewis' paths for 500 lb. Virginia Currency, and when a very considerable distance ahead, he fell down and broke his neck.

He left some very superior racing stock behind him; his owner kept him alternately as a race and covering horse. He died at 20 years of age, and stood in Halifax Co., N. C., in 1781.

John Goode.

Bowlaway

C. A. Q. Running Horse:

Got by Young Monkey—Liberty (son of I. H. Dove)—I. H. Bashaw—I. H. Dabster—I. H. Childers—I. H. Bulle Rock.

Va. 1798   Edward Wyatt, Sen.

N. B. Bowlaway was a capital racer, and won immense sums of money. He was a dark chestnut horse, well formed, 14 hands 2 inches high.

Broomtail

C. A. Q. R. Mare (full sister to the C. A. Q. R. M. Sweeping Tail) bred by the late Joseph John Alston, Esq. of Halifax County, N. C.:

Got by the I. H. Old Janus—F. A. R. Mare Poll Pitcher by I. H. Old Janus—C. A. R. H. Lee's Old Mark Anthony—C. A. Q. R. H. Brinkley's Peacock—I. H. Silver Eye—I. H. Old Monkey.

N. C. 1818   Hon. Willis Alston,
                                        Late member of Congress.

Club Foot

R. H. Bred by the late Col. Thomas Eaton, of Halifax County, N. C., and foaled about the year 1778:

Got by I. H. Old Janus—I. H. B. Old Fearnought—I. H. Janus—I. H. Jolly Roger—imported mare Mary Gray.

Club Foot was an excellent quarter of a mile racer, a chestnut horse, without any marks, 15 hands 1 inch high, very substantially formed, and a horse of prodigious powers; he was carried out to the western country, his forefoot was considerably injured which grew to a great size and occasioned him to receive his name.

Dappled John

A dappled horse, very well formed, about 15 hands high, very compact, with heavy hindquarters; a fine head and very short neck, and one white hind foot, also a few white hairs on his face. He was a very fleet horse for a short distance, and had excellent bottom.

Got by Lloyd's Travellar—I. H. Old Janus—I. H. Old Janus.

N. C. 1825   Titus Moore.

HARLOT

F. A. Q. R. M.:

Got by Old R. H. Goode's Bacchus—Coelia by R. H. Goode's Babram—I. H. B. Old Fearnought—I. H. Old Janus—C. A. R. H. Brinkley's Peacock—I. H. Monkey—I. H. Silver Eye—I. H. Silver Eye—I. H. Monkey—imported mare.

N. C. 1813   Charles R. Eaton.

KING TAMMANY

F. A. Q. R. H. (Old) bred by the late Mr. William Jackson, of Franklin Co., N. C.:

Got by Eaton's Little Janus (son of the C. A. H. Meade's Old Celer)—C. A. R. H. Lee's Old Mark Anthony—I. H. B. Old Fearnought—I. H. Old Janus—Brinkley's C. A. R. H. Peacock—I. H. Old Janus—I. H. Old Jolly Roger—I. H. Old Monkey.

N. C. 1814   Wm. Jackson.

He died at 18 years of age.

Maj. Cordie Ferrell rode the above horse a great many races, and informed the Compiler that he was the strongest and swiftest horse of his size in the world; he won immense sums of money.

N. C. Jan. 1821   Cordie Ferrell.

Description of Old King Tammany: "He was a pale sorrel horse with a streak in his face, and two white hind feet, beautifully and substantially formed, and possessed great muscular powers; 14 hands fully high."

ONE EYE

C. A. Q. R. H. a beautiful blood bay horse, lightly formed, 15 hands and 1 inch nearly high:

Got by I. H. Old Janus—I. H. Old Janus—I. H. Old Davis—I. H. Jolly Roger.

Martin Co., N. C., 1798   Wm. Williams, Senr.

N. B. This horse was a very celebrated racer indeed; he got capital racing stock for short distances only. He lost an eye by accident when a colt, and received his name from this circumstance.

N. C.   Giddeon Alston.

DUN HANCOCK

This stallion is owned by W. B. Warren of Hockley, Texas, and is one of the great sons of Joe Hancock. Mr. Warren's nephew, Johnny Warren, astride.

JIMMIE ALLRED

This Quarter stallion is owned by Helen and Maxie Michaelis, and is a grandson of Joe Bailey, and a great-grandson of Hickory Bill. He was quite a race horse in his day.

BOB CROSBY ROPING
Bob Crosby retained the title World's Champion Steer Roper, at Carlsbad, New Mexico, where these two shots were taken. Here you see some great Quarter Horses working. The dark horse holding the steer down is the world famous roping horse June Bug, one of the greatest modern Quarter Horses.

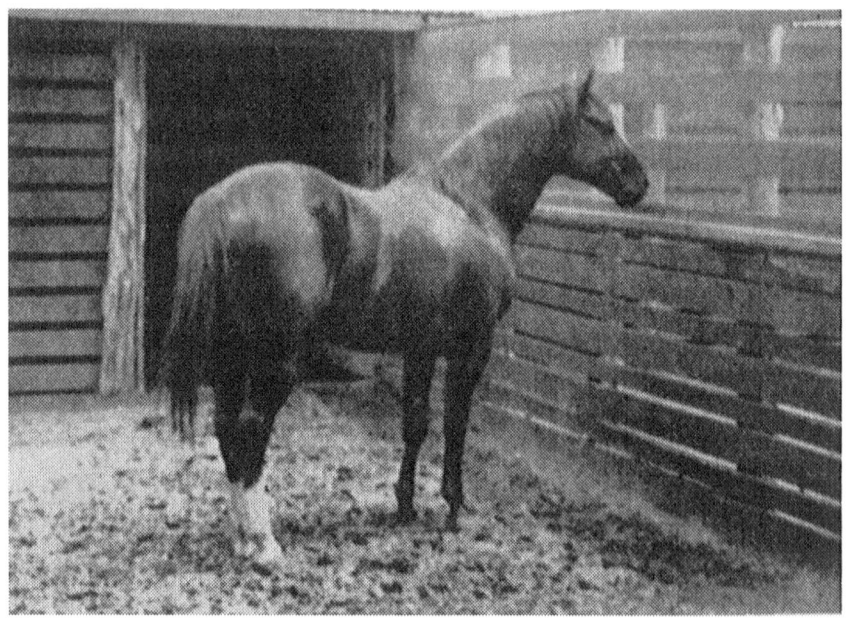

DUTCH McCUE
Dutch McCue is one of the greatest colts Jack McCue, by Peter McCue, ever produced. Until he was turned over in a trailer he was a real running horse. He is owned by R. L. Underwood of Wichita Falls.

Paddy Whack

F. A. Q. R. H. foaled in 1778, formerly the property of Mr. John Goode, senr. of Mecklenburgh County, Virginia (commonly called "Little Twigg"):

Got by I. H. Old Jolly Roger—I. H. Old Shock—I. H. Sober John—Both imported by the late Col. Baylor.

Paddy Whack was matched by the late Mr. Henry Delony, of Mecklenburgh County, Virginia, to run against the C. A. Q. R. H. Old Twigg, at that time the property of Mr. Goode, as aforesaid, one quarter of a mile, at Nicholson's Quarter Race Paths, in said County, for 80,000 lbs. of tobacco, which race was won by Twigg.

The same day, the same persons made a bet of 100,000 lbs. of tobacco, to be run for in 6 months after, by the same horses, which race was won by Paddy Whack, beating Twigg inches on the same paths. These races were run in the year 1786.

Signed,   John Goode,
                                           Henry Delony,
                                           Henry Cradle.

Attested in Mecklenburgh County, Va.
April 6th, 1798.

Paddy Whack was a capital quarter racer in Mecklenburgh, and the adjacent Counties in Virginia, also in the States of North and South Carolina, to which places he was frequently carried for the express purpose of racing. He was a race horse of the first class for quarter of a mile, half mile, and mile races. He won immense sums of money, beating all the best race horses of his day—so that frequently when taken to strange places, his appearance was altered in order to procure races to be made upon him, as he was always feared by his competitors wherever he went or was known.

Va. 1790.   Edward Davis.
A true copy.

Peacock

F. A. Q. R. H. (Old) pale sorrel horse, elegantly but very lightly formed, possessing great power and strength for a horse of his make; 15 hands fully high:

Got by I. H. Old Janus—his dam was an imported mare, brought from Old Spain. N. B. This horse was foaled the property of Joseph John Alston, Esqu. of Halifax Co., N. C., in 1760, and transferred to the late Mr. Brinkley, of that County and State, and afterwards was called "Brinkley's Peacock." He died in the State of South Carolina, aged 26 years.

He was one of the swiftest quarter of a mile racers in America of his day, and won upwards of $40,000.

N. C. 1772. Joseph John Alston.

Poll Smiling

C. A. Q. R. M. a red sorrel mare, very well formed, with a blaze face and two white hind legs above her hocks, 13 hands 2 inches high, bred by the late Mr. John Goode, Sen. of Mecklenburgh Co., Va.; foaled in 1774—Mark Anthony—I. H. B. Old Fearnought—I. H. Old Jolly Roger—imported mare Mary Gray.

N. C. 1778. Wyllie Jones.

Sir Walter Raleigh

A dark bay horse, compact in form, and very beautiful, 15 hands high; he got a handsome and serviceable stock of horses, and also many capital quarter racers. He was bred by the late Col. John Whittaker, of Halifax Co., N. C.; foaled in 1779:

Got by the C. A. R. H. Lee's Old Mark Anthony, (the very last horse of his get)—his dam, by C. A. R. H. Spottswood's Apollo—A. R. H. One Eye—thoroughbred mare.

Jan. 3, 1829 Gen. the Rev. Eli B. Whittaker.

Spadille

(Old) C. A. Q. R. H. formerly the property of the late Wyllie Jones, of Halifax County, N. C.:

Got by I. H. Old Janus—imported mare Selim, by the Godolphin Arabian—Large Hartley mare, got by Hartley's blind horse—Flying Whig, by William's Woodstock Arabian—Points, by the St. Victor's Barb—Whynot, (son of the Fenwick Barb).

Northampton County, North A. Jones.
Carolina, March 20th, 1770.

TWIGG

(Goode's Old) C. A. Q. R. H. a beautiful bright bay horse, heavily made, with a large blaze face, and two white hind feet, 14 hands 1 inch high, very compact, highly formed, and possessed with great muscular powers, symmetry, action, and strength:

He was a quarter of a mile race horse, of the very first class. His speed was unknown to all his competitors, and whenever he was equally matched, he was universally successful. He won immense sums of money and hogsheads of tobacco. We have heard his breeder at different times assert that he was the strongest and the swiftest horse in the universe, for three or four hundred yards, and that it was impossible for any horse in existence to beat him unless he was made to carry heavy weights, or run a distance beyond one quarter of a mile. He rarely ever was beaten, unless from some of the foregoing cases. The only horses, in his prime of life, which generally attempted to contend with him, were Polly Williams, and Paddy Whack. He ran upwards of a dozen times with both the above horses, and never was beaten but once by each, owing entirely to the weight which he carried, which was generally 108 pounds.

He beat Polly Williams 8 times out of 9, for from 80,000 to 100,000 pounds of tobacco. He also beat Paddy Whack eleven times out of twelve for very large sums of money and tobacco. He was run against Paddy Whack at Nicholson's Quarter Race paths, in Mecklenburgh County, in the State of Virginia, for 80,000 pounds of tobacco, when he beat him ten feet, (with the greatest ease) in one quarter of a mile. He had at two or three different times beat him for from 30,000 up to 50,000 pounds of tobacco. Another race was made in the year 1786 to be run at the same place for 100,000 pounds of tobacco, Twigg carrying twenty pounds more than Paddy Whack, which was won by the latter, beating him only 18 inches.

He was bred by the late Mr. John Goode, Sen. of Mecklenburgh County, Va. (commonly called Little Twigg); foaled in 1778.

Got by I. H. Old Janus—C. A. Q. R. mare Puckett's Switch, by I. H. Old Janus—I. H. Old Janus—I. H. Old Janus—I. H. Old Jolly Roger—I. H. Old Monkey.

Mecklenburgh Co., Va. April 6th, 1798.
1798.   John Goode, Sen.
                                                     Henry Delony.

I do hereby certify that I am very well acquainted with the celebrated quarter of a mile racer called Goode's Twig. He was a racer of the very first class, for from three hundred yards to one quarter of a mile. He never could run a farther distance. He beat all of the most celebrated racers which could be brought against him, and was universally successful unless when run over the above distance, or compelled to carry heavy weight. He was the swiftest horse on earth for three hundred yards, carrying a feather, and he has run against the very best horses in America, three hundred yards, and beat his competitors one hundred and twenty feet in that distance.

Mecklenburgh Co., Va. April 6, 1798.
Jan. 19, 1787. Edward Davis.

WILLIAMS, POLLY

F. A. Q. R. M. a red sorrel mare, very highly formed, with beautiful fore parts and a very high goose rump, ragged hips and very narrow behind, a very large blaze face and all four legs white, bred by the late Mr. Peter Williams, of Dinwiddie County, Va.; foaled about the year 1774:

Got by the C. A. R. H. Lee's Old Mark Anthony—I. H. Old Janus—I. H. B. Old Fearnought—I. H. Jolly Roger—imported mare Mary Gray.

N. B. This celebrated mare never produced a foal.

The following account of Polly Williams, we have obtained from various sources, and from people of the strictest integrity in every instance:

"A race had been made upon this mare, between old Mr. Davis and the late Mr. Henry Delony, of Mecklenburgh County, Virginia, for 500 lbs. Virginia Currency. Polly had distinguished herself by quarter racing so often, that finally no races whatever could be obtained against her. Old Mr. Davis kept her as a riding horse and lent her out to a relation. During the term of the loan she was parted with, (unknown to her proprietor,) to the aforesaid Mr. Delony, who, immediately after, went over to old Mr. Davis' house and challenged him for a race, saying he had a mare which could beat any mare he owned, or could be obtained in the United States, for 500 lb. Virginia currency, play or pay. Mr. Davis immediately confirmed the bet. They both mounted their horses and went over to a neighbor's house in order to draw the articles of agreement and to deposit the money. After these preliminaries were completed, the parties separated, Mr. Davis to send into Virginia for Polly Williams and Mr. Delony to put her in order for the race. Old Mr. Davis, on arriving at the house of the person to whom he lent his mare, was astonished at learning that his celebrated mare was traded away, and more particularly to the very man, whom, of all others, he was unwilling should own her, and more especially, as he was not quite certain he had lost both his mare and money. Mr. Delony, on the other hand, paid every attention to Polly, in order to prepare her for the race. But, most unfortunately for him, indeed, the weather had been rainy and cloudy for several days, so that she could not be taken out of the stable, either for the purpose of exercising or watering her. At length the atmosphere became serene once more, and between dusk and night she was led out to the stream in order to drink. During the time of declining her head to the water, a rifle ball was shot through it. This act was always supposed to have been done by a negro man of Mr. Davis' by the name of 'Ned.' Mr. Davis claimed the stakes and got them."

It was a practice in Virginia and North Carolina in giving the pedigree of a horse to give only a few crosses, particularly on the sire's side. Many Virginia pedigrees traced back to the earliest imported horses end off with "famous imported mare." This practice caused great distress among the compilers of the first studbooks. The source records of the well-bred matrons brought to Virginia before the Revolution are incomplete and in part doubtful. The fecundity of these mares is astounding. There are only twenty-one immigrant matrons whose pedigrees and history can be given as authentic. The fact of the matter is that the "thirty-eight" pioneer sires brought to Virginia before the Revolution were bred mostly to native Virginia and Spanish mares to produce the superior race of horses described above. Of these thirty-eight imported English horses there were about fifteen which proved to be prepotent sires of Quarter Running Horses. In the pedigrees of the Celebrated and Famous Quarter Horses will be found the names of nearly all of the stallions imported prior to the Revolution. The stallions whose names appear most frequently in these pedigrees, and to whose blood the Quarter Horse is deeply indebted, are described below:

Bulle Rock

Imported into Virginia before the Revolution in 1730, and foaled about the year 1718:

Got by the Darley Arabian—Byerly Turk—Lyster Turk, out of a natural Arabian mare.

Virginia, 1735. (Signed) Samuel Patton.
1736. Samuel Gist.

N. B. He traces back to the following dates: 1689, 1686, and 1584.

Jolly Roger

Jolly Roger was the first horse that gave distinction to the racing stock of Virginia. His performances on the English turf, and that of his pedigree, are recorded in the name of 'Roger of the Vale.' After he was imported into this county he took the name by which he is now known; he was foaled in 1741, and commenced covering in Virginia about the year 1748. He was got by Roundhead, who was by Flying Childers, who was by the Darley Arabian. The dam of Roundhead was the famous 'plate' mare Roxana by the Bald Galloway, the dam of the celebrated racers and stallions Lath and Cade by the Godolphin Arabian. The dam of Jolly Roger was got by Mr. Croft's famous horse Partner, the best racer and stallion of his day, his grandam by Woodcock—Croft's Bay Barb; Makeless; Brimmer; Son of Dodsworth; Burton Barb mare.

JANUS

Janus was imported into Virginia by Mr. Mordecai Booth, of Gloucester County, Va., in the year 1752; his dam was got by old Fox, (whose name stood eminent in the English pedigree,) his grandam by the Bald Galloway. Although Janus partook of every cross in his pedigree calculated for the distance turf horse, yet his stock were more remarkable for speed than bottom. Janus, from his shoulders back, was considered the most perfect formed horse ever seen in Virginia, by the most skilful connoisseurs; he was remarkable for roundness of contour, strength of articulation and indicating great powers and stamina in his whole conformation.

His stock partook of these qualities in an eminent degree, and for thirty or forty years they were considered as a "peculiar stock," as they invariably exhibited even in the third and fourth generations from the old horse, the same compactness of form, strength and power. The Janus stock have exceeded all other in the United States for speed, durability and general uniformity of good form; and more good saddle and harness horses have sprung from them than from any other stock.

CELER

Celer was justly considered as the best son of old Janus, as he propagated a stock equal in every quality to those of the stock begotten by his sire. He was bred by Mr. Mead of Virginia, and foaled in 1774, and died in 1802, aged 28 years.

As the pedigree on his dam's side is not generally known, I will give it here. The dam of Celer was got by the imported horse Aristotle, a brown bay, finely formed, fully 15 hands high, bred by Mr. Gladen and got by the Cullen Arabian, his dam by Crab, his grandam by Hobgoblin, great grandam by the Godolphin Arabian, out of a famous mare called White Cheeks.

MORTON'S TRAVELLER

Morton's Traveller, imported horse, contributed in an eminent degree to the improvement of the turf stock of horses in Virginia. He was a bay horse, foaled about the year 1748, and was a covering stallion at Richmond Court House, Va., as early as the year 1754. He was bred by Mr. Crofts, at Raby in Yorkshire (who was the fortunate breeder and owner of some of the first horses in England) and was got by his famous horse Partner, who was a grandson of the Byerly Turk, and was himself the grandsire of King Herod. The dam of Traveller was by Bloody Buttocks (an Arabian) Greyhound; Makeless; Brimmer; Blace's White Turk; Dodsworth; Layton Barb mare. Morton's Traveller was bred from the best running stock in England in that day; the famous Wetherington mare was full sister to Traveller; she bred Shepherd's Crab and other capital racers.

MARK ANTHONY

Mark Anthony was foaled about the year 1763, and did not exceed fifteen hands in height, and was a horse of beauty and intrinsic value, whether viewed as a racer or stallion. In the former character he was not excelled by any horse of his day, being "remarkable for his swiftness," having at the same time good wind, enabling him to run four-mile heats in good form. In the latter character he stood deservedly celebrated, and propagated a stock which were held in the highest estimation for their various valuable qualities, whether for the turf, the saddle or the harness—Mark Anthony got Collector out of Centinel, and Monarch out of a thorough bred mare, and Romulus out of Valiant.

FEARNOUGHT

Fearnought holds the first claim prior to the day of Medley, and is therefore entitled to the palm in preference to any stallion that has preceded him in giving the Virginia turf stock a standing equal to that of any running stock in the world. The blood which flowed in the veins of old Fearnought must have been peculiarly rich in those qualities which make up the conformation of the race horse, as not only the whole stock got by Fearnought run well, but also his sons and his grandsons were remarkable for generally getting good running stock. There was also strength and stamina universally pervading the Fearnought stock, to which may be added good size, that made them the best distance horses of their day. The fact is that the Fearnoughts run well all distances, and the old horse stood higher than any other horse on the continent for getting racers; and he got more of them than any other—he was also the sire of more fine stallions than any other horse of his day.

Old Fearnought was bred by William Warren of England, and foaled in the year 1755. He came out of Mr. Warren's fine brood mare "Silvertail," and was got by Regulus, the best son of the Godolphin Arabian. Regulus, when six years old, won eight King's plates. He never was beat, being very superior to any horse of his day.

Medley

The stock of old Medley may justly be ranked as among the most remarkable and valuable that have ever signalized themselves on a Virginia race course. This stock of horses lacked nothing but size to have made the best racers in the world; and yet their want of size was not manifested on the turf; as their ability to carry weight exceeded that of any other stock; they were also remarkable for good wind or bottom, for fine limbs and good eyes, more than any other race horses that have been bred in Virginia. These qualities resulted in this stock (and were more peculiar to them than to any other) from the close proximity of the points of the hips to the shoulder, from the uncommon solidity of their bones, the close texture of their sinews, and the build and substance of their tendons, which always enabled them to carry the highest weights, and to endure the greatest stress on their bodily powers. To these qualities may be added their uncommon purity of blood, derived from their sire Old Medley, who was one of the purest blooded horses ever bred in England.

Gimcrack

Gimcrack, the sire of Medley, was one of the most remarkable horses of his day in England. He was a grey, and called the "little grey horse Gimcrack," foaled in 1760, got by Cripple, a son of Godolphin Arabian. Gimcrack was one of the severest running and hardest bottomed horses that ever ran in England; although small, yet his ability to carry weight was very great, for he frequently gave the odds as high as 28 pounds, and he continued on the turf until 11 years of age, thereby showing his uncommon hardiness of constitution and firmness of limbs which he richly transmitted into the veins of Medley.

OTHELLO

Othello, a beautiful black, fifteen hands high, very strong, was got by Mr. Panton's Crab, in England, out of the Duke of Somerset's favorite brood mare. Othello covered in Virginia, on James River, in 1761, and was a most capital stallion. He got Selim and the dam of Mark Anthony.

SELIM

This beautiful and valuable stallion was a dark bay, a little rising 15 hands high, was got by Othello, (commonly called Black and all Black) whose name was Old Crab. The dam of Selim was a beautiful mare of that name, got by the Godolphin Arabian and full sister to the celebrated horse Babraham of England. Selim was a tried and approved racer, and a stallion of deserved celebrity. He stood in Virginia from the year 1770 to 1780, and propagated a valuable race of horses.

MONKEY

Was formerly the property of Lord Lonsdale, and imported (we have been informed) by the late Nathaniel Harrison, Esq. of Brandon, Va., at 22 years of age, in the year 1747; foaled in the year 1725.

Got by the Lonsdale Bay Arabian—Curwen's Bay Barb—Byerly Turk, out of a natural Arabian mare.

Monkey got an excellent stock of horses in America, and upwards of 25 colts were produced by him. He died in 1754, as we learn.

SHARKE

A brown horse, bred by Mr. Pigot; foaled in 1771:

Got by Old Marske—his dam by Old Snap—Marlborough, out of a natural Barb mare, in the Duke of Marlborough's stud.

N. B. Marlborough was full brother to Babraham, and the imported mare Selima, (dam of Selim).

Old Sharke won 12,187 guineas, in England. A cross of him is excellent in American mares, both for speed and bottom, lastingness and ability to carry heavy weights.   Thomas Goode.

A study of the descriptions, portraits and histories of the earliest horses of the turf show that when our racers ran longer distances and carried greater weight, their forms were more compact and muscular. The standard by which the physical power of the English racer was tested was lowered by the Jockey Club in 1809. Four-mile heats, with weight as high as 168 pounds, had ceased to be run before the end of the 18th century.

The performances of the earlier racers were greater than those of the modern Thoroughbred. The former remained considerably longer on the track. The 4-mile and 6-mile heats which were held at New-Market during the 17th and 18th centuries demanded a combination of speed, stoutness and structural power in the horse. The desire to increase the given speed of the race horse and to breed for that single characteristic has resulted in the gradual deterioration of the Thoroughbred as a general utility animal. The increase in the given speed of the racer has been attended with a change in conformation and structure and diminished muscular power. This change in the hardiness and endurance decreased about the second half of the 19th century. The single quality of given speed possessed by our modern racer is not a substitute for the union of speed, stoutness and structural power possessed by the old horses and which is absolutely essential in the Quarter Horse.

It is not the writer's purpose to condemn the modern Thoroughbred but to emphasize the fact that the early Quarter Horse and the early Thoroughbred were similar in blood lines, conformation, hardiness and endurance; and that the present day Thoroughbred which may possess Quarter Horse conformation and which has the ability to transmit desirable characteristics, will prove most useful to the Quarter Horse breeders in fixing the type.

The Thoroughbred occupies the most prominent position of any breed in the world. Through the veins of all of our light breeds flow his blood. To him the American Saddle Horse, Standard Bred, Hackney, steeplechaser (formerly half Thoroughbred), Trotters and Coach horses owe their existence. And the early importations of blood which later became the Thoroughbred, greatly improved the colonial Quarter Horse.

There are today in the United States about 50,000 registered Thoroughbreds. The business of racing is gigantic. About 13,000 horses run annually, for over $10,000,000.00. It is a regrettable fact that so few of these racing machines are capable of producing the ideal type of horse for working cattle and general use on our rough ranges. There are, however, some outstanding individuals of this great equine family which possess Quarter Horse conformation, and characteristics, and some have proven their ability to produce Quarter types when bred to selected mares. The Army Remount Service has done some wonderful work in providing Thoroughbred stallions and supervising breeding activities throughout the country. The breeders who have the use of these Remount stallions are producing wonderful half breed horses of Thoroughbred type, for use in the Cavalry and Artillery. The Army needs more and better Thoroughbred sires to carry on the Remount breeding plan. The ideal type of Remount stallion is 16 hands to 16 hands 2 inches in height, weight 1,100 to 1,200 pounds. But they are very difficult to obtain. In the Remount Service there are about 700 Thoroughbred stallions, and of these there are 113 in Texas. The Texas stallions average slightly over 15 hands 3 inches in height, and there are only a very small number of them of the Quarter Horse type and capable of producing top cow horses. The great majority of the produce are not the cattleman's and the stock horse breeder's ideal.

The King Ranch, under the careful guidance of Robert J. Kleberg, Jr., President, has produced a special type of cow horse through crossing Thoroughbred and Quarter Horses. He has followed a scientific and systematic plan of mating superior individuals, both breeds, that reproduce characteristics desirable in the cow horse; and he has fixed a type of all-purpose horse. Mr. Kleberg's breeding program, which was launched 22 years ago, has been followed with a great amount of interest by horsemen and breeders throughout the Southwest, and is recognized as an outstanding accomplishment in careful selective breeding. There are also other breeders who are doing commendable work along these lines.

The Quarter Horse has retained all of the characteristics which made him famous. He can still run a quarter of a mile faster than any other breed of horse. He can put on his working clothes and do a great variety of jobs and do them better than any other breed, and he has not deteriorated at his work. He still possesses hard muscles, substance, action and ability to carry heavy weights. He has retained his great vigor and his form because he has lived and worked under conditions nearest to those of nature. Throughout three centuries his rugged individualism has not diminished.

Quarter Horses are an economic necessity. The demand for this type of all-purpose horse for polo, pleasure riding, rodeo contests and for handling range cattle is constantly increasing. This horse has a brighter future than that of any other breed of utility horse.

The American Quarter Horse Association and the Quarter Horse Camp Meeting Association were organized by a large group of prominent men composed of outstanding cattlemen, horse breeders and Quarter Horse enthusiasts throughout the Southwest, for the purpose of establishing and perpetuating a breed of great equine utilitarians. These associations will succeed in their object and purposes, because they are controlled and sponsored by men of honor and integrity, men who are working unselfishly to gain recognition for this horse, and to elevate him to a high position among the other families of the equine aristocracy.

The Quarter Horse in Mexico
By HELEN MICHAELIS

THE QUARTER HORSE is a race horse bred to run a short distance. The Mexicans call him *Media Sangre* (half-Thoroughbred) or Corredor de distancia carta (short distance race horse). He probably originated in the United States but he developed in Mexico. He traces to Thoroughbred, Arab and Andaluz blood. His dam was a Mexican Quarter Mare. She made the present-day Quarter Horse possible. Her kind are still plentiful; a small, short-coupled, short-legged, well-muscled, clean-legged horse with speed and "bottom."

Mexicans are natural horsemen and racing has a long history in the Land of Mañana.

It has been said that the first Thoroughbreds in the New World were shipped to Mexico, but as the foundation sires of the Quarter Horse they were first used in the United States. Between 1870 and 1880 many good Thoroughbreds were imported to Mexico, at which time the Jockey Club of Mexico was organized. *El Jockey Club de México* was founded by General Don Pedro Rincon Gallardo, Senor Don Eduardo Rincon Gallardo y Rossa, Duque de Regla, and Don Pablo Escandon. Mexicans have always preferred short races so *El Media Sangre* soon took the place of the Thoroughbred as a race horse.

El Media Sangre was produced by crossing fast, broad, well-muscled Thoroughbred stallions with native Spanish mares, carefully chosen and preferably mountain raised. Both the stallion and the mare were chosen with much care. Because the stallion predominates he was as well bred as was possible to secure. From the sire the colt gets bone, nerves, firmness of tendon, speed and disposition. His best breeding age is from seven to fourteen years. The mare must be of good origin, fast, sound, broad and of good color. She is the model and produces her own kind. She should be larger than the stallion. She gives her colt color and something of her conformation. Her best breeding age is from four to twelve years. These simple rules the Mexicans followed to develop a horse that is a distinct type and of a straighter line of breeding than many other breeds of present-day horses. Accepting the foundation stock as one-quarter Arab, one-quarter Andaluz and one-half Thoroughbred, one might say the present-day Quarter Horse has lost all the characteristics of the Thoroughbred except his unusually large heart girth and his tendency to be low mounted. His speed he inherited from all sides. One cannot say a Quarter Horse is part Thoroughbred any more truthfully than he can say an American Saddle Horse is part Thoroughbred. All horses had a common origin and the blood of the noble Arab flows in the veins of all light horses. So potent are the characteristics of the Quarter Horse that his blood is recognized in a horse that contains as little as one-eighth Quarter Horse.

Duque De Regla, Marques De Guadalupe, described a typical Quarter Horse as follows:

QUARTER HORSE MEN

This picture shows Jack S. Casement and R. L. (Lee) Underwood on the Triangle Bar Ranch in Colorado. Both are directors of the American Quarter Horse Association.

PANCHO

Pancho was owned by W. B. Warren of Hockley, Texas. He was sired by Paul L., and his dam was by Little Joe.

MARGIE
Champion Quarter mare at Tucson and Fort Worth, 1941. In racing form and she can shade 23 seconds in the quarter. She is owned by Marshall Peavy of Clark, Colorado.

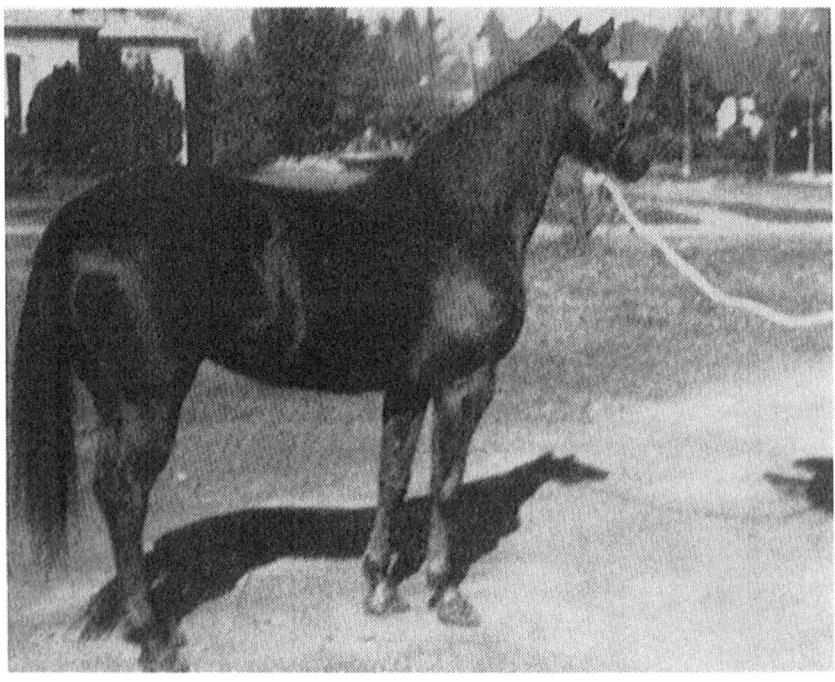

FANNIE
Fannie is the outstanding rodeo mare owned by Peggy Minnick and has been ridden by her at rodeos all over the country, including Madison Square Garden, New York. Miss Minnick is the daughter of J. H. (Jim) Minnick of Crowell, Texas.

"Poll: wide, well raised and round on both sides.
"Forehead: wide and full in front.
"Face: short, wide and straight.
"Ears: thin, slightly arched and short. They must be well set, slightly forward and constantly in motion.
"Eyes: big and full of life.
"Nostrils: black, wide and dilated.
"Neck: thin, fairly long and well-shaped.
"Mane: fine, brilliant and preferably falling on the left hand side, all of it.
"Back: as straight as possible.
"Kidneys: wide and short.
"Tail: full, long, fine and well carried; set well at the top and thin at the ends. It should be carried close to the buttocks.
"Chest: protruding and wide.
"Shoulders: long and sloping.
"Forearm: well muscled and long.
"Canon: short and firm.
"Pastern: strong, fine, clean and short. A 45-degree angle is considered perfect.
"Hoof: hard, thick, dark and round.
"Croup: wide and round.
"Height: about *un metro y cuarenta y cinco centimetros* (57.0865 inches, or approximately, 14½ hands).
"Disposition: quiet, but with plenty of ginger."

A first-class Mexican Quarter Horse can run 100 varas (92⅔ yards) carrying 90 kilos (198.4140 pounds) in 6 or 7 seconds. A horse is fast that can run 300 varas in 14.05. The usual distance run is from 200 to 400 varas (185⅓ to 370⅔ yards). Only two horses are run in a single race and the track used is the same kind that was used in the United States when the Quarter Horse was first popular. The track is two lanes, each two meters wide, with a mound furrowed down the center. Posts are conveniently placed to keep out spectators. Each horse must stay in his lane. A pistol shot or a flag is the usual signal to start, and it is the getaway that counts, as all races are run from a standing start. There are two judges, one at either end of the track. The winning horse must have his front feet across the line unless otherwise specified in the written agreement, which is called a *vale*. The jockeys ride without hats but with large handkerchiefs tied around their heads. They ride barefooted and in shirt sleeves. Heavy betting is done on the side. As much as 50,000 pesos changes hands in a single race.

The written agreement between the owners of the two horses has already been referred to as a *vale*. The *vale* contains the names of the owners of the horses, names of the horses and a detailed description of each horse, the place, date and hour of the proposed race, the wager, which must be deposited with a reliable business house, the weights to be carried and the manner in which the jockeys must dress. The time limit in which the horses are to start, usually thirty minutes, is stipulated, and if at the end of the thirty minutes the horses have not started the judge decides the additional time allowed. The lane in which each horse is to run must be stipulated in the *vale*. It is sometimes agreed the winning horse must win by his entire body *(con blancos)*, showing daylight between his tail and the nose of the other horse. If the winning horse is to win by *manos claros* it is to say half his body must cross the line. If one of the horses should die or become disabled before the race the winnings go to the owner of the other horse. This manner of winning is called *ganar a pico torcido*.

Jalisco is the home of the fastest Mexican Quarter Horses. They are there known as *Los Altos*.

Most of the best Quarter Horses in the United States have sooner or later found their way to Mexico. Of the most famous Quarter Horses in Mexico in the past forty years some were bred in Mexico and some in the United States. They were: El Chaqueta Azul (Blue Jacket), El Nudo, El Columpio, El Gacho, La Tapatia, El Please, El Jose Chiquito (Little Joe), El Spade, El Vulcano, El Leonel, El Valentino, El Limberg, El Tirano, La Bonita and El Lidio.

Each of these horses was valued at not less than 3,000 pesos and some were valued at 7,000 pesos.

Mexico is a big country and is the home of some of the best horses in the world. The border country has many "scrubs," but the interior is rich with super-horseflesh. Within two hundred miles of the border one sees horses in a *remuda* that should be on the tracks. In whatever part of Mexico there is money, short races are won and lost. There was never a horse that could not be beaten and there was never a *caballero* that did not love racing.

PART FOUR

Utility, Performance, Characteristics

Explanation for Speed

By BOB DENHARDT

IT IS EXTREMELY DOUBTFUL if those 17th century breeders in the English Colonies knew just why the horse they developed had such an exceptional burst of speed. Probably they cared less. They just mated their fastest horses, producing in a hundred years a horse which defeated the first English Thoroughbreds imported into America. They still do today, some two centuries later. It was the writer's privilege to see in West Texas one Sunday just a few weeks ago, a Thoroughbred fresh from Kentucky defeated in a short race by a Steel Dust stallion, to the extreme, and it might be added, financial, embarrassment of the Kentucky owners. It is a fact well known to Quarter Horse breeders that their best horses can run a standing start quarter faster than the average Thoroughbred will run any single quarter in his race. This fact is hard for the "long horse" man to accept, consequently no little money has changed hands. There is a very good reason for the speed which lies dormant in this horse. Those very features which mark him as awkward to the Easterner contribute to his superiority in his own particular race—a short one. Examination and explanation of these features are the purpose of this article.

The reason for the Quarter Horse's unusual success in the short races is due to his peculiar conformation. Even a casual observer can distinguish two types of saddle horses by their conformation—one chunky, the other slender. These types are well illustrated by two modern breeds, namely, the Thoroughbred and the Quarter Horse. (See illustration chart facing page 118.) It is probably well to acknowledge at this point the wide variation of individuals. By a discussion and comparison of these types the advantageous features of each may be discerned.

The legs of a horse, like the legs of a desk, are his support. Like a desk, the longer, the less the stability; the shorter, the more power and stability. In horses the center of weight is far forward, lying, in fact, immediately behind the shoulders. Consequently, the forelegs must support most of the weight, hence the functions of the forequarters, support; the function of the hindquarters, to propel. When a horse is standing the base of support is a rectangle, outlined by the horse's feet; at a walk it is triangular as one foot is up; at a trot or pace the base of support is a line as only two feet are down. In a run or gallop the base of support is a point. Thus, as the speed increases, the points of support decrease, and there is a corresponding decrease of stability.

The instability of the horse increases with his speed and is caused by his weight being so far forward that in action it is almost over his forelegs, whose function of support is then at a maximum. In walking the horses pushes backward against the ground with his hind feet and the center of weight tips forward. If he didn't advance a forefoot he would land on his head. Walking is merely a succession of interrupted falls. In the other gaits there is the same backward thrust with the hind feet, but as the thrust is greater, the stride is longer, and the shock and effort of recovery greatly increased.

It is evident that a horse, to move forward, must thrust at the earth, the force of the thrust coming almost entirely from his hind legs. The farther forward the center of weight, the longer the line from the hind foot to center of weight. This line is technically known as the line of thrust. (See illustrative chart facing page 118.) The more nearly this line approaches the horizontal, the greater the forward motion. This can be illustrated by imagining a gun being fired. If you hold the gun pointing almost directly overhead the forward motion toward a target 100 yards away and on a level with the gun will be very slight. On the other hand, if you hold the gun horizontally and toward the target, the forward motion toward the target will be at a maximum. In short, the more energy the horse exerts in propelling himself forward and the less he pushes or lifts up, the greater the speed.

Of paramount importance, then, in the speed of the horse, is the placement of the weight. The farther forward the center of weight, the longer is the line from hind foot to the center of weight, or line of thrust, and the more nearly it approaches the horizontal. The less the angle of thrust, the faster the horse will go, for more power will be utilized in forward movement and less energy exerted in mere weight lifting. Like a man with a wheelbarrow, if the load is near the handle he must lift it each step, while the load over the wheel allows all energy to be expended in the forward push.

The above facts bring out the function of the forelegs of a horse—support of the weight. This also shows why a horse is more apt to tire his forelegs (than his hind ones) which carry the load. The same explanation shows why a horse should not be run down hill because then all of the weight hammers on his forelegs. The jar caused by the horse's weight being thrown on his forelegs is absorbed by three primary features. The first is the hoof mechanism. Without going into detail, the following things occur when weight is placed on the hoof, contraction of the hoof at the toe-wall coronet, sinking of the sole, expansion of the heels, and sinking of the bulbs of the heel. This manifold foot mechanism absorbs concussion somewhat similar to an automobile tire. The second feature absorbing the jar is the slope of the pastern, acting like the spring of a buggy. And, thirdly, there is the sloping shoulder (angle between humerus and forearm, scapula and humerus) which also acts as springs. Anyone who has stood with straight legs on the bed of a hay wagon traveling on a rocky road knows the effect of the jar. Bend your knees and your teeth stop chattering. The angles of your legs then act like the pastern and shoulder slope of a horse, absorbing concussion.

The above somewhat detailed description of the essentials of speed in a horse, namely, line of support, line of thrust, and absorption of concussion are all essential to the full understanding of the Quarter Horse's unusual speed. Bearing these factors in mind, it is possible to see why, in the types of horse represented by the Thoroughbred and the Quarter Horse, each has definite characteristics. The first, sustained speed, and the last, unusual bursts of speed and unusual ability to maneuver quickly at full speed.

Let us take each in turn, point out the principal characteristics and abilities due to his build, then compare them. The Thoroughbred, with his slender shoulders, neck, and head, carries less weight over his forelegs than any other breed. Thus, at speed the concussion on his forelegs is at a minimum. Extremely powerful muscles in his croup, thigh and gaskin provide his propelling power. Because of the lightness of his forequarters he can sustain speed. His long, slender legs also increase his speed, although they decrease his stability.

The Quarter Horse is extremely heavy in front, packing his weight almost directly over the forelegs. This causes his peculiar stance, a tendency to "camp under," with forelegs sloping back to support his weight. Because of this tremendous burden his forelegs are very short and extremely well muscled inside and out to withstand concussion. The Quarter Horse must support from one-third to one-half more weight per hand on his forelegs than the Thoroughbred. His strength for sudden speed becomes his chief drawback for distance running. The weight proves too much strain on his forelegs for sustained action. However, his powerful and stocky legs, increasing his stability, give him his unsurpassed maneuverability. He can stop and turn at speeds which other horses find impossible. The Quarter Horse carries more weight, farther forward, and his stocky legs put the center of weight lower, than the Thoroughbred. This decreases his line of thrust until it more nearly approaches the horizontal, the facts which make for speed in a horse. This explains why the Quarter Horse can outrun any other breed in short races. It also explains his principal weakness from a racing man's point of view—his inability to sustain his run. His unusual weight so far front tires him rapidly at his fastest gait. The Thoroughbred, because he is lighter in front, making the concussion on his forelegs less, has sustained speed.

As thrust and stride are increased, the shock and effort of recovery are increased proportionately. Granting thrust and stride to be developed to a maximum, then the sole remaining way speed can be obtained is by lowering the line of thrust. This can be accomplished in only one way, by moving the center of weight forward, which in practice is equivalent to increased weight, similar to the Quarter Horse. Jockeys, realizing this, ride far forward on the horse's neck, thus throwing more weight forward, decreasing the line of thrust and hence increasing speed. This, however, would necessitate shorter legs to absorb the increased shock and concussion, not only reducing sustained action but shortening the long legs, another factor in speed. So we have the Thoroughbred, with his long legs decreasing stability and its counterpart, "maneuverability," but by the same means increasing his speed. His light weight per hand lessens the shock and effort of recovery, but acts to raise his line of thrust. This decreases his speed, but by the same means allows sustained action.

The two extremes can never meet in the same horse. The closest approach is the Arabian, whose conformation differs radically from either. His peculiar features allow exceptional individuals of his breed occasionally to outperform either a Quarter Horse or running horse in their own field. However, the average Thoroughbred has a greater sustained speed than the Arabian, just as the average Quarter Horse has a greater burst of speed and greater stability.

Breeders must breed for one or the other. Line of thrust can only be lowered by putting more weight on the forelegs, and even when they are shortened to give the needed stability they cannot for a long period sustain the shock. Quarter Horse breeders cannot breed for less weight in front, for if they do, the line of thrust is raised and speed lost. The legs are also lengthened and stability and maneuverability lost. Both types are necessary and both the best in their field. The Thoroughbred on his track, the Quarter Horse on the stock ranch. As a "dogging" or roping horse the Quarter Horse has never been excelled. A flashing burst of speed to overtake the animal, an almost unbelievable ability to stop or turn at full speed, make his type incomparable when working on a ranch or in a rodeo. His speed on a short track has been traditional in the East since Governor Nicholson legalized racing in Virginia in the 1600's and in the Southwest since the famous horse, Steel Dust, defeated a Texas horse soon after the Civil War.

Is the Quarter Horse a Thoroughbred?
By BOB DENHARDT

OFTEN you hear people say casually that Quarter Horses are just Thoroughbreds. More often than not this happens when some of the more outstanding horses are mentioned. To them this settles any and all discussion on the matter. Some thought on the subject indicates that the two are distinct types, each with a customary conformation and ability. A real understanding of the purpose and characteristics of the Quarter Horse and the Thoroughbred eliminates any tendency to confuse the two. Certain criteria may be applied to both horses, and if kept in mind, distinction is normally easy.

Quarter Horses at present are not strictly a breed as they have no studbook or registry, and so they will be referred to as a "type." Thoroughbreds are a breed in this respect. All good breeds have the power of consistent reproduction of like ability and conformation. Therein lies the crux of the situation—and the knowledge of which factors allows the horseman to differentiate one from the other. Man is responsible for the differences which occur. Years of use at one particular type of activity, years of selective breeding with but one end in mind, produced the abilities and conformation found in each animal. The

Thoroughbred has been bred with but one motivating idea—sustained speed. In the early days it was not uncommon for the horse to run three 4-mile heats. Fastest bred to fastest begot faster until today the Thoroughbred is the unchallenged leader in the running field. His body changed during this period also. His weight per hand dropped considerably. This was due to three things—his legs got longer, his head and neck lighter, and his bone more refined. All these helped increase his speed. The first lengthened his stride, the second reduced the shock and concussion on his forelegs, and the third eliminated the bulk of excess weight. They became the greyhounds of the horse world.

There were really two factors which developed the Quarter Horse. Need of utility with speed. Time and place determined which was paramount. The Quarter Horse has always been the ordinary man's using-horse. Owner bred, owner trained, and more often than not, owner raced. These things are important to understand his characteristics of utility and speed, just as it was necessary to understand what was wanted when the Thoroughbred developed. To be useful on the frontier and the ranch the horse has to have certain characteristics, namely, weight, a certain rugged power, and ability to live off of the country. There is no Derby or Santa Anita when and where the Quarter Horse developed. The Quarter Horse was matched and raced where his owners met, for a hundred yards or as far as they could see an opening, seldom over a quarter of a mile, hence his name. For short distance racing a tremendous burst of speed is more valuable than sustained action. The Quarter Horse evolved muscle for this, which the owner used during the week. A heavier bone also appeared to support his weight. He developed short forelegs (noticeable particularly in cannon and pastern) which lowered his angle of thrust and increased his speed. He developed tremendous rear quarters, muscled to the hocks, and a shoulder and forearms bulging with muscle. With these he could break from the line running his fastest at the drop of the hat. The Quarter Horse added weight to his neck and head. The center of weight was consequently placed more to the front of the horse and thus lowered the line of thrust and so increased his speed. In short, this helps in much the same way that the jockey's position aids the running horse. However, his weight, particularly in the forequarters, is a drawback in regard to sustained speed. He cannot touch the Thoroughbred in this line, but his short, stocky legs give him greater stability, and what is important on a cattle ranch, ability to maneuver. The Quarter Horse can stop and turn at speeds which the Thoroughbred (with his longer and lighter bones and weaker joints) finds impossible.

So we have the two types, Thoroughbred and Quarter Horse, which the years have molded into two forms which the horseman can recognize by their conformation. Turn a real horseman into a corral in which there is a Quarter Horse, a Thoroughbred, an American Saddle Horse, and a Morgan, and he will point them all out to you. In this matter of conformation there are of course wide differences in individuals, even of the same blood.

FROSTY

Frosty is probably one of Balleymooney's greatest sons. He is owned by Chick Logan of Tucson, Arizona, and was raised on the Triangle Bar Ranch of Jack Casement. He has been champion stallion almost every place shown.

QUARTER HORSE OFFICIALS

The above picture shows, reading from left to right, W. B. Warren, President of The American Quarter Horse Association; J. H. Minnick, Director and Inspector, and Bob Denhardt, Director and Secretary, at the Stamford Cowboy Reunion in 1940.

YOUNG COLD DECK

Young Cold Deck was the foundation sire of the Blake Quarter Horses. He was sired by Old Cold Deck and brought to Oklahoma from Tennessee by Coke Blake.

LITTLE JOE III

This is the great South Texas Quarter stallion which was sired by Traveller and whose dam was by Rondo. He sired some of the best, including Zantanone, Ada Jones, Jim Wells, Cotton Eyed Joe, Joe Moore, and many others. He also had a racing record seldom exceeded.

There are other yardsticks by which a Quarter Horse is sometimes measured. By one definition, any running horse whose best distance was under a mile would be a Quarter Horse, whether he looked like one or not. Given enough time and the consistent mating of the fastest animals, and there would develop a horse whose conformation could be similar to the present Quarter Horse. The performance is important, but just because an exceptional individual can match a certain breed's best performance does not mean that he belongs to that breed, or that his get will be as good as the get of the breed. Some Arabian horses have defeated Thoroughbreds in races, but they are always the exception. Just because some particular horse is built like a Quarter Horse does not mean he can match the performance of a Quarter Horse or that his offspring will look like them. This is applicable to all breed types. Individual conformation or performance never of themselves make a breed. This is what was meant when earlier the statement was made, though occasionally it is possible for a horseman to confuse a Quarter Horse and a Thoroughbred. When they look alike, or will perform alike, it is possible to become confused. Then parents and offspring must be taken into consideration in determining the exact family to which the individual belongs.

There is one other factor which has led to misunderstanding amongst horsemen. That has been the occasional false registration of Quarter Horses as Thoroughbreds. This is particularly true since the tracks have been closed to other running horses. One of the greatest Quarter

Horses of all time was Peter McCue. He apparently never lost a race. Twice he ran the quarter in 21 seconds flat (unofficial), as fast a time as is claimed by any horse. The second time was in 1901 at Harlem race track in Chicago. After the sixth race Peter McCue was stepped from the quarter pole to the stand in 21 seconds flat. Fifteen watches caught him, including such men as Sam Hildreth, Rome Respess, Jim Arthur, Ed Trotter, Uncle Jim Grey, J. F. Newman, and Fred Woods. He was ridden at the time by H. N. Smith of Fort Worth and carried 122 pounds. Peter McCue was a Quarter Horse. A glance at his picture shows his conformation is not what is considered good Thoroughbred type. His best speed was in short distances and this would indicate him as a Quarter. His colts were short horses almost without exception. Therefore, knowing just these three things, one might reasonably call him a Quarter Horse. The confusion enters when men who do not know these things claim he was registered in the Jockey Club. Peter McCue was registered, but from the above it might be assumed his ancestry was such that he should not have been registered. There are in my possession the following documents regarding his breeding, all of which indicate he should not have been registered: A letter from the owner of one of his most famous sons, Harmon Baker. A letter from his owners to the man buying another famous son, Buck Thomas. A letter from one of the family who went up and bought the real sire of Peter McCue from his breeders; a letter from the man who bought him and had him at his death.

Most livestock men accept the fact that there are occasional false registrations in breed associations. Probably the Thoroughbred is not an exception, and it may be inferred that some Quarter Horses have been registered as Thoroughbreds. The Quarter Horses claimed to be Thoroughbreds are either falsely registered, or not Thoroughbreds. This is true because to be a good Thoroughbred a horse must be able to sustain speed; a Quarter Horse cannot. To be a Quarter Horse, he must have short, powerful legs, immense muscled rear quarters (standing often higher than his withers), a heavy head and neck, loaded forearms and sloping croup. Good Thoroughbreds lack these conformation characteristics. They cannot have them and be good track horses, the principal purpose for which they were (and are) bred.

There were several other thoughts along this line worth noting. If horses were bred for generations to produce distance runners, like the Thoroughbreds, where did this horse come from that could run, as the old saying goes, only as far as he could hold his breath? Wouldn't it seem funny for consistent breeders to produce these animals with a radically different conformation, one that demanded the bridle to be shortened and the girth to be lengthened? If they are the same breed, why is it that each cross of Thoroughbred blood on a Quarter Horse lengthens his distance? The answer is plain.

There is one fact which both Quarter Horse and Thoroughbred men will have to admit. Many great horses have been a Thoroughbred-Quarter cross. That excellent horseman, Major E. G. Cullum, who is in many ways the severest critic of the Quarter Horse, admits that the Quarter Horse blood in the Thoroughbred has produced some of the really great polo horses. He finds fault with Quarter Horses in several places. He dislikes their sloping back and flat withers and feels they lack a good saddle back. He claims their gaits are rough and says they lack the stamina and endurance of the Thoroughbred. There is undoubtedly some truth in his criticism, but Quarter Horse men will not admit that there are any faults which cannot be eliminated or if they are a type characteristic which are not offset by other superior qualities.

All Quarter Horses do not have poor withers and selection and intelligent breeding will develop adequate withers in the future. A sloping back they may always have to some extent, as it is vital to their center of weight and angle of thrust. Raise these and some of his speed is lost. This slight angle is not noticeable under a stock saddle. Some of the gaits of many Quarter Horses are rough. An important factor which makes some gaits rough is his short and often rather upright pasterns. The great weight per hand that the Quarter Horse carries necessitates stronger pasterns than the other saddle breeds. The deep sloping shoulder on the best Quarter Horse offsets this feature, but mount a Quarter Horse which has a straight shoulder and the true impact of Cullum criticism will be felt. The right kind of Thoroughbred blood helps a Quarter Horse in developing better withers and a more sloping pastern. It also gives him a little more distance at his fastest gait.

Major Cullum also faults them on lacking stamina and endurance. It is true they cannot, due to their peculiar conformation and weight placement, keep up their fastest speed for long distances. However, that does not mean they cannot work on the range all day and then "coyote lope" home all night. They will outwork any other type and do it on less feed. They might be compared to a heavy man who cannot run at high speeds as long as a light man, but at his own speed the large man can outwork the light, and do it day after day.

It is equally possible, though, to fault Thoroughbreds from a rancher's point of view. When they are slender, long-legged and light, with small bones, they are not ideal cow horses. They need to pack more weight per hand, they need a little heavier bone in their legs to stand up under heavy work in bad country. They should be a little less high strung, and they should come down a little closer to the ground. These things can all be accomplished in several ways. The quickest is to add a little Quarter Horse blood. Another is to take them off the tracks and let them mature on the ranch. These faults of the Thoroughbred are not against him as a distance runner where he has no equal, but as a ranch horse, for which he has not been bred.

A little research will show that the Quarter Horse has been a distinct type since Colonial days, before any important English importations of Thoroughbred blood were made. It will also show that in Edgar's Studbook horses which were later considered by Bruce as foundation horses for the American Thoroughbred were originally entered as Quarter Horses. Today, except for the cowman, the rodeo man, and certain Western polo breeders, all of whom just could not find a better horse for their particular purpose, the Quarter Horse has had no consistent breeding. Its blood has become diluted. It is time that an organization was formed to preserve and improve this horse which has no peer when it comes to working cattle or running a short race.

The Social Significance
By DAN D. AND JACK S. CASEMENT

THE PRIMARY WEALTH of the pioneers of the Southwest was purely pastoral. For untold centuries before the coming of the white man the Indian had unconsciously based his primitive economy on the vegetation indigenous to his habitat. The uncultivated fruits of the soil and the herbivorous animals, which subsisted on such natural forage as the country afforded, supplied him with all the elements essential to his constantly hazardous existence.

Obviously, if civilized men were to survive in a country previously inhabited only by wild men, it would be wise if not instinctive on their part to adopt, in large measure at least, the principles underlying the economy of their wild predecessors. But the white man's inherited impulse to enhance his so-called social security promptly led him to modify this economy in many ways. Most important of the alterations which he imposed on the native way of life was the semi-domestication of his meat supply. Cattle, originally introduced by the Spanish explorers, were substituted in his system for the buffalo, deer and antelope on which the Indian had chiefly subsisted.

In this process the native horse played a part no less important than that of its rider. The Mustang of the Southwest, descended from the desert strains of Northern Africa, introduced by the conquistadors, had undergone trying experiences in America which had fitted him perfectly to the uses to which he was put by the pioneers of Texas.

Four hundred years he shifted for himself in a country where the rigors of Nature permitted only the toughest and smartest of his species to survive. His apprenticeship for working cattle had been fully served with the reckless-riding Comanches in running buffalo.

Without the help of the Spanish Mustang the early Texans, in establishing themselves in their new homes, would have been constrained to adapt to wild western beef production the milk-maid arts of their abandoned civilization. The creation of wealth would have entailed largely the slow and unromantic process of plodding behind the plow. For certainly no strain of horses in North America had inherited character and capacity equal to the demands made on the Mustang by the early Texans in accommodating their lives to the natural economic set-up they found in their new environment.

It was the little native Spanish horse which enabled the

brush-hopper of South Texas, at the end of the war between the States, successfully to hunt and to bring under his control the semi-wild, long-horned cattle which roamed from San Antonio to the Gulf and to the Rio Grande.

It was only by dint of the unequaled qualities of this horse that wild wealth was accumulated, assembled into herds and trailed to distant markets. It was this little horse which headed the sudden stampede, swam the swollen streams and surmounted every peril and hazard of the long journey.

It was, too, an equally remarkable race of men whose will to live hard and dangerous lives matched in every respect the spirit of the horses they rode.

Since the passing of those days when the West was new, with the disappearance of the Mustang and of the men who rode him, much of that which was most distinctive and admirable in our national character lives only in tradition. But fortunately there are still men who treasure that tradition and conform their lives to it as closely as modern conditions will permit; men who deeply revere and naturally emulate in their own characters and conduct the shining examples of their pioneer Pappies.

Happily for them, people's lives are still very largely dependent upon the pastoral industry, and, in the West, cattle are still worked with horses. Happily for them, too, most of the characteristics that made the Mustang a wonder-mount for cow work have survived in his worthy successor, the Quarter Horse.

The origin of this truly American horse is undoubtedly almost as remote as that of the Mustang. He evolved rather out of the recreational inclinations than from the economic necessities of his creators, the early Cavalier colonists of the Atlantic seaboard. Unlike their Puritan neighbors to the north who required a multi-purpose horse that could make shift at plow, road cart or under saddle, practical Southern gentlemen tilled with their long-eared mules, but rode, if possible, runners. The famed Justin Morgan was the product of Puritanism.

For those Southerners horse races at distances greater than a quarter of a mile were impossible because they had no courses longer or faster than those afforded by the main street of the village or the level surface of a small clearing in the forest. To fit the requirements imposed by these conditions they produced by careful selective breeding a distinctive American race of horses which has never been surpassed for those qualities which the highest type of American men, as exemplified by the pioneers of the West, valued most highly in their equine companions which shared the work and play of their hard and hazardous lives. In every feature and lineament the true Quarter Horse reveals the qualities most prized as the highest physical attributes in Man himself—courage, muscular strength, endurance, agility and speed. A keen intelligence and the tenacity of a bulldog are his also by rightful inheritance.

With the boys of his creators this horse came over the Blue Ridge Mountains at an early day and eventually found his way to the Southwest. It is probable that some Barb or Arab blood had originally entered his life stream through horses brought to Florida by the Spaniards. At any rate, in his initial nick with the Texas Mustangs, their mutual product revealed the congenial characteristics of true soulmates.

Heir to a more refined culture than that reflected in the development of the Mustang, the Quarter Horse stamped the progeny of their mating with a smoother, less angular form and a more kindly eye than the mother's. She, however, contributed to the invaluable qualities of their offspring an inherited cow sense that never could have been imparted by blood nurtured on the Atlantic Coast.

The modern successor of the original Quarter Horse is the natural beneficiary both of all the fortunate circumstances incident to his eventful history, and of the sterling qualities of the men to whom he owes his being and his subsequent improvement. Of all that is admirable in human character, the world can show no better examples than those depicted in the lives of the men who subdued the Southwest to the uses of modern civilization. In this hard process their essential and most dependable ally was the horse. As they were cow hands incomparable, it is not surprising that they should have evolved nothing less than a wonder horse to fit their exacting needs. Fortunately for America, the standards by which those men lived survive in large measure in their descendants, while the qualities of the mount they found fully adequate to their demands survives today in the Quarter Horse.

But, during a recent decade and a half even the descendants of pioneer stock slipped toward the decadent. The spiritual affliction which drove men to set "standards of living" above their standards of conduct reflected from a mechanized civilization striving to shift into high gear direct from compound low. The practical side of horseflesh was forgotten, and equine husbandry was practiced primarily as a mark of social distinction. Governmental subsidy of Thoroughbred breeding was all that was needed virtually to complete the job of weaning the affection of a lot of old-timers from their once cherished "bulldogs," who had stood by them in sickness and health, labor and levity, and to splice them to a fickle-headed, thinner-thighed equine seductress. Now the pendulum is swinging back. Men are finding out that devotion lavished upon descendants of stock that has for generations been developed solely for the circular, velvet-smooth, artificial environment of the mile track is not often rewarded and seldom returns either cash dividends or increased character. The Quarter Horse is coming back as it again becomes recognized that he is the only fit companion for men who are fit to face down the newer, more subtle problems of mechanized life.

Such men remember that, after all, the task of cutting wild weaner yearlings on a top mount is the greatest privilege that a man can be given. They remember that the days of he-man hilarity were those of the unorganized rodeos, like that never-to-be-forgotten Christmas-to-New Years celebration in Southeastern Utah in which all the horses were played out by too many scorings and dead heats, so that bets had eventually to be settled by foot races, bottles and bullets.

The true cavalier is reasserting himself. Those who sincerely prefer a stirrup to a clutch pedal, those sage brush students of environment and heredity who realize that horse culture is a give and take deal in which the man learns and develops as much as his mount, those who know that, in a cow country, one is spiritually as well as physically half afoot on anything but a Quarter Horse. They know that the most specific antidote to this short-shift, machine age is a pre-dawn to after-dark set in a saddle. They know that organized Quarter Horse husbandry, if run right, will yield as big a crop of human values as horse flesh.

Worth His Salt

By ALBERT HAND

THIS ARTICLE is written in defense of the famous Quarter Horse—an animal having had much to do in the vast development of our country, an animal that has stood up well through all sorts of hardships and retains great popularity even today in our hard-riding Western country. The Quarter Horse is still used by the hundreds on cattle and horse ranches, for pleasure and trail riding, and is the only type of roping mount worth its salt in the fastest of all equine sports, the American rodeo!

Knowing the authentic history of just a few of the many achievements accomplished by these horses, it is indeed a mystery to us how any person can, as several have, condemn the Quarter Horse as being such a worthless type of mount. Yet there are a few people who have lit on these horses with very abusive language in articles written by people claiming to be horsemen.

I am sure that deep prejudice is the cause for these people taking such action in regard to the Quarter Horse. I feel that these same people are wrong in the entirety, and because I am extremely familiar with this type of saddle horse, having handled and ridden them under most conceivable conditions, I will say this about them: Quarter Horses are, on the average, the fastest sprinters, possess more intelligence, stamina, sure-footed and "catty" action and *all-around handiness* and ability than any other type of saddle horse. Their records prove such. And records must guide us, not the false belief of some unknowing person.

The true Quarter Horse can match accomplishments with any type of mount and he will come out with a high marking when the final accounting is made. Only recently did two Quarter Horses carry, alternately, their rider from Nocona, Texas, to Treasure Island in San Francisco Bay, a distance of 1,750 miles, in the short time of twenty-three days. These two horses wore a heavy Western stock saddle and carried a rider tipping the beam at 160 pounds. Their trail led over mountain, plain and desert, through a swirling dust storm and blistering heat.

Another feat gaining much glory for the Quarter Horse took place at last year's horse show at Phoenix, Arizona, when Bob Crosby rode his Comet horse to first place in a "stock horse reining contest." Comet won the blue ribbon hands down and he showed against some of the best cow horses in the entire Southwest.

Quarter Horses have made possible the setting of all present-day rodeo arena records. Cowboys riding these horses have been able to lower the calf roping record to *eleven seconds flat.* The steer wrestling record has been dropped to *three and two-fifths seconds.* It would have been impossible for these records to be lowered as they have if the men who made them had not been riding the fastest sprinters to be found. And the Quarter Horse is such an animal!

Quarter Horses have been identified with the fast game of polo since its beginning in this country. The ability of these horses on the polo field is stated plainly in the report of the match game played at Oklahoma City between a Kansas City team, riding Thoroughbreds, and a team made up of cowboys mounted on ponies of distinct Quarter type. The official report of the game reads: "The game was on! The Cowboys outgamed and outrode the City team. Those rugged little Quarter Horse cow ponies, under the guiding hand of master horsemen, darted here and there, making the shortest turns with lightning-like rapidity. The final score was 11 to 2 in favor of the Cowboys."

Almost half a century has passed since a cold-blooded

Quarter Horse ran a quarter mile distance at Butte, Montana, to set the world's record of 21¼ seconds. The record still holds! Even with scientific breeding of late years there has been no horse produced to as much as equal the mark, much less better it.

The above statements cannot be disputed because they are facts. These facts should serve to convince all persons that while some may not like the Quarter Horse for their personal use, those same animals still rate a high marking in any line of equine activities.

Several famous families of the western Quarter Horses carry such names as Steel Dusts, Cold Decks, the Blake horse, Copper-Bottoms, Printers, Go-Alongs, Rondos, Billys, and Skunk Tails (so named because of the many white hairs in their tails, regardless of body color).

These families have produced not a few animals which have made their mark as polo mounts, jumpers, famous roping and bulldogging mounts, short distance race horses, famous cow and stock horses, and several highly educated trick, posing and *manège* horses.

Fireball, as true a Quarter Horse as was ever foaled, was crowned champion polo pony several times over at horse shows along the Pacific Coast. Rosky, another of these Quarter Horses, was hunted in the East, where he won many blue streamers, later going to France, where he played some mighty fast polo. The mare, Coleen, owned by the United States Army, was the undisputed winner of the Grass Rider's Grub Stake at Fort Riley, Kansas. Peanuts, also owned by the army, was one of the greatest all-around jumpers ever ridden into a show ring. The little sorrel pony, San Bonita, was sold as an international polo mount several years past. And Clipper, a fine Quarter Horse, was declared Medal Pony of the 11th Cavalry Club of Monterey, California. Stranger, the red-roan pony belonging to Mike Hastings, was the greatest bulldogging mount of all time. Legs, the rope horse belonging to the champion contest roper, Jake McClure, was considered one of the greatest animals to ever carry a cowboy after a wild steer.

You have just read a few records and accomplishments of true Quarter Horses which prove them exceptionally "handy" at whatever task they might be asked to perform. And how any person can say that the Quarter Horse is an inferior mount is something we wonder about. Yet such has happened of late.

I won't even try to explain the origin of these animals. This thing has been attempted, with failure, too many times before. But I will say the Quarter Horse was popular and in great demand during the very early days of this country. History mentions them as racing animals of the Planters and Country Gentlemen of Virginia and the Carolinas.

Neither will I dwell on the conformation of the Quarter Horse, for any person criticizing the animals would be certain to pick an inferior one when casting his opinion. That would hardly be fair, as all strains of horses produce such an animal occasionally. Therefore, a short summary of the build, characteristics, and actions of the true Quarter Horse should, I feel, prove him to be an ideal mount for most any purpose where sure-footedness, stamina, speed, and intelligence must be had.

Quarter Horses seldom exceed 15 hands, and weigh from 900 to 1,100 pounds. They are deep through the chest and breast, are extremely well muscled over their entire body and legs. A true Quarter Horse stands with all four feet well under his body, has a good straight hind leg and a stance of appearing to lean slightly forward on his front quarters. They possess finely shaped and very strong hoofs, a well-shaped head on a short, well-proportioned neck. They have a back that most any saddle will fit, a fine coat, and are as clean-limbed as any known breed. Also, the Quarter Horse is the quickest of foot in close quarters of any type of mount. They stop and turn while other horses are thinking about the act. And their intelligence for stock or cow work cannot be equalled. Too, they are of rugged constitution, exceptionally "light feeders," and are willing to give their best when called upon.

I have ridden them after wild horses, after cattle, over desert and mountain trail, across swirling rivers when it was pitch dark, over ice-coated hillsides, through ankle-deep mud, and in rodeo arenas over the entire country. I have schooled them as polo mounts, and, because they have everything—intelligence, stamina, sure-footed action, and much general all-around handiness—Quarter Horses are, for my money, the best type of mount that a man can ride. They will take you there and bring you back. I have never seen one of them quit when the going got tough, and as the late Will Rogers once remarked, "A Quarter Hoss is good enough for me!"

Losin' One's Shirt

By WAYNE GARD

NOWADAYS, to lose one's shirt at the races means merely to go without pin money for a week—or, at worst, to put a gold watch in hock for a fortnight. But in the day of the Quarter Horse, when "the turf" meant virgin prairie sod instead of a meticulously graded and sprinkled track, the wagerer was in real danger of going home in his undershirt. Worse than that, an unlucky cowhand might even have to lug his saddle back to the ranch and wait until payday before he could buy a new mount of his own.

When he backed a winning horse, on the other hand, he might come into sudden possession of a new Stetson, a store-bought suit, a wool blanket, or a buffalo robe. If any of these articles came from Indian hands, he likely would spread them over ant hills for a day or two to make sure they were deloused; but he was not particular what he took in on wagers, since hard money was scarce and those who had it seldom ventured much on the Sunday afternoon races.

Demand for polo mounts recently has caused breeders to search for survivors of the almost extinct Quarter Horses—so called because they were bred and trained to run a quarter of a mile. Crosses of Thoroughbreds with Quarter Horses have produced ideal polo ponies, with the intelligence and endurance of the former and the small size and quickness of the latter. Some of the offspring from such crosses made at the famous King Ranch, in Texas, have distinguished themselves both in international polo matches and on fast race tracks.

In the Southwest, revived interest in the Quarter Horse has led breeders from eight states to meet in Fort Worth and form a Quarter Horse Association. This step will give the old favorite of the cow country a new standing in the equine world, but it hardly can bring back the prairie races in which the Quarter Horse covered his name with luster.

Attaining fame without benefit of any jockey club, the Quarter Horse claimed no ancient lineage. Obscure beginnings make it impossible to trace the origin of this type, never fixed any too definitely at best. Since Quarter Horses were racing in Kentucky by 1800, the theory that they were descended in part from mustangs of the Western Plains is hardly convincing. Another story has them derived from the wild horses of Chincoteague and other islands off the Virginia coast—perhaps Arab steeds left there by Spanish ships in distress. A third explanation is that the Quarter Horse obtained his Arab strain from Spanish mounts in Florida or the West Indies.

Yet lack of pedigree did not deter the Quarter Horse from becoming a superb sprinter. One of the most compactly formed steeds ever known, the typical Quarter Horse stood only 14 to 15 hands high, but often weighed 1,000 to 1,200 pounds. With short legs, thick body, and knotty muscles, he was more chunky than handsome; but on a short stretch he could show amazing speed. He responded instantly to his rider's signals, and in the range country was in strong demand as a cow pony.

Since they had no race tracks available, pioneer Kentuckians often matched their horses on public highways or village streets. Soon this practice became a nuisance that brought as many complaints as the unseemly display of stallions in public squares. By 1800 the towns were imposing a fine of five dollars for racing in a public thoroughfare. In 1798 the trustees of Lexington ordered the collection of fines for street racing, and in 1821 Kentucky's lawmakers made racing on the highways subject to a ten-dollar penalty. But highway racing continued in the remoter parts and spread to the frontier states. As late as 1874 a Kansas editor suggested that the only way to prevent horse racing in a street would be to plow a deep ditch across it.

By 1850, when Kentuckians had turned to blooded stock, prepared tracks, and longer races, quarter racing was taken up on the Southwestern frontier, where, in the '70s, it reached its highest development. Texans imported Quarter Horses from Kentucky, Tennessee, Illinois and Missouri, and developed the type with new strains. The less formal matches were held on the open prairie, with cowhands and village youths as spectators. The more important ones were announced in the newspapers, and often drew an attendance of a thousand males. On occasion, the town's "soiled doves" drove out in fancy carriages to patronize the event; but other women generally stayed home from all but the biggest matches, and parsons frowned upon the races and attendant gambling.

For the impromptu races of the prairie turf no grandstand was needed. Each spectator came on horseback and remained in his saddle to watch the matches, his face shaded by the wide brim of his hat. Often the mounts of the patrons formed solid lines along both sides of the course. Usually some of the onlookers came on ponies hired from livery stables, and this circumstance gave village cut-ups opportunity for a bit of fun. One spirited youth would snatch the reins from an unsuspecting race fan and toss them over the horse's head. At the same moment, his confederate would give the livery horse a hard swat on the rump. The startled horse would then tear out for his stable in town, the rider clinging on as best he could and trying ineffectually to stop the rushing steed.

Scrub races of this kind had few standing rules; separate agreements usually were made for each match. The typical race was a match between two horses, often representing rival towns; but sometimes more horses would compete. At the starting point, the judges would line the horses with a tree or post or some other fixed object, such as the end of a wagon. Care had to be taken in choosing judges, since charges of foul play often led to fights. One Indian judge, determined not to be tricked at the finish line, stretched across the court a light rope he had just smeared with war paint. He ruled that the winning horse would have to show a mark of red paint to claim the prize.

Several methods of starting the ponies were used. One

was by pistol shot, and another was by the "lap and tap." In this case, the horses were led about fifty feet back of the starting line, where they whirled and began running. If the judge found them sufficiently close "in lap" as they crossed the starting line, he "tapped them off" by shouting "Go!" Otherwise, they would have to make a new start.

A third method of starting, common in Texas and the Indian Territory, was by "ask and answer." Under this plan, the starter would ask, "Are you ready?" When he heard the competing riders answer "Yes," he would shout, "Go!" and the match would be on. For some of the more important races, the start would be made from chutes constructed of narrow poles; but for the more ordinary sort of prairie pastime, these were not essential.

Once the ponies were off, the spectators threw their hats into the air and set up shouts that drowned out the sound of flying hoofs. Often confusion would arise before the outcome could be determined, and sometimes there would be disputes over alleged infringement of rules. In most cases, of course, wagers were paid promptly; but when the losers were Indians, always there was the hazard that they might run off with the stakes or return after dark to steal back what they had lost.

Of all the strains of Quarter Horses, that of Steel Dust was by far the most famous. Today the original sire of that name belongs more to folklore than to history, since his origin is unknown and many of the stories about him are conflicting. Yet there is no doubt that such a stallion existed in Texas in the '50's and later and that he gave rise to one of the fleetest lines of Quarter Horse stock.

Larger than the ordinary Quarter Horse, Steel Dust was nearly 16 hands high and weighed about 1,100 pounds. His name may have come from his color, described variously as blood bay or gray roan. Though one account attributes his origin to Missouri, he is generally believed to have been brought to Texas from Kentucky, possibly by way of Missouri. Some think he was imported to Texas for a match with a Lone Star champion.

The most romantic explanation is that Steel Dust, though brought to Texas by a Kentuckian for what was intended to be a temporary round of racing, won so steadily that the cow country refused to give him up. The Texans paid off their lavish bets, this story goes, but visited the barn at night to see that a horse able to make such winnings was not wasted by being returned to Kentucky.

Better documented is the story that Steel Dust was sired by Harry Bluff and was brought to Texas in the early '50's by two farmers who lived at the southern edge of Dallas County, about three miles below Lancaster. These were Thomas McKee Ellis, who had come from Illinois in 1845, and his son-in-law, Jones Green. Steel Dust's first Texas match was against Monmouth, owned by the Stiff family of McKinney, well known in the racing world of that day. For this race, courts were closed in Sherman, and even in distant Jefferson; and sportsmen and political bigwigs came from many quarters to witness the big event.

So many visitors poured into McKinney the day before the race that the Foote House was turned over to the ladies and the men were told to find what sleeping space they could in homes or stores. Steel Dust arrived with a bodyguard of half a dozen men and enough backers to take up all the local bets. The Dallas stallion won this exciting race; and, as a result, many McKinney people had to use something else for money until they could sell their next crops.

But Steel Dust's racing career was short. In 1855, then three or four years old, he was owned by Green and another son-in-law of Ellis, Middleton Perry. In that year people gathered in Dallas from far and near to witness a quarter race between Steel Dust and another celebrated horse called Shilo, brought from Tennessee in 1849 by Jack Batchler, a blacksmith who lived across the line in Ellis County and who found more interest in the turf than in his forge.

The account of this race given many years later by Batchler's son states that Steel Dust, eager for a start, reared and plunged in the chute. In making his leap to clear the stall, he struck the wall and ran a splinter in his shoulder, which disabled him. Shilo then was galloped over the course, and his owner claimed and received the forfeit. Blinded from this injury, Steel Dust never raced again; but his renown was such that he was in wide demand for breeding for many years, during which he had several owners in turn.

M. H. Raburn, whose father, Bill Raburn, was one of the later owners of Steel Dust, gives a variant account of the famous 1855 race, newspaper reports of which were lost in a Dallas fire. As he heard the story, Steel Dust's trainer sold out the match but neglected to inform the jockey of the deal. As the race was about to start, the trainer caused Steel Dust to rear in the chute and fall to his knees. But the jockey pulled him up and, in spite of a bad start, won the race.

Whatever happened on that Dallas track in 1855, Steel Dust became the most famous sire in the Southwest for a generation. His more notable offspring included Gray Dick, owned by the Thomason family of Denton County and winner of many matches from Texas to Tennessee, and—perhaps the fleetest of all—Gray Alice, owned by Jim Brown. When C. A. Williams and John Reynolds enlisted in the Confederate cavalry, they proudly rode Steel Dust colts. Every time these Texans happened to be thrown with a new command, they would match their ponies in quarter races at the first opportunity. In this way, they kept themselves supplied with pocket money for tobacco and other luxuries throughout the war.

Inevitably Steel Dust has had hundreds of horse owners making false claim of his lineage for their broomtails, but lines stemming unquestionably from him have given fine accounts of themselves on the race track and at the roundup. Clay McGonigle, for two decades one of the world's top steer ropers, did his best work with a Steel Dust mount. Many a ranchman still boasts that his ponies are of Steel Dust descent.

Best remembered of all the horses that carried Steel Dust blood in the quarter races is Jenny, usually known as the Denton mare. Perhaps her name would be less green if the youth who owned and raced her had not later become a famous brigand and train robber, but Southwestern legends and one of the most widely known cowboy songs will carry to generations to come the story of Sam Bass and his Denton mare.

This mare was a two-year-old when Bass, then a cowhand and teamster in Denton, saw her racing possibilities and bought her. That was in the fall of 1874. By spring, Jenny had outrun every contender in the county and was becoming the talk of sportsmen over a wide section. So Sam threw up his job, became a professional racing man, and hired as a jockey a featherweight Negro, known as Dick, who was able to handle the mare better than anyone else.

This jockey made several innovations. While most of those who rode in the quarter races used light saddles, Dick rode bareback with only a smear of molasses on Jenny's sides to help him stay aboard. He also discarded the usual bridle for a simple rope halter called a hackamore. The mare seemed to understand his every word or touch; he had only to pat her neck to stop her after crossing the finish line.

At the Denton track, Sam introduced a peculiar method of starting. Believing his mare could gain an advantage by starting downhill, he built—with the help of a friend and the Negro jockey—a dirt mound at the track's starting line. This elevation, at its highest point, was two or three feet above the surrounding level. Whenever an opponent objected to his use of this mound, Sam conceded a slight lead to the rival horse. Old-timers still point out a vestige of this mound on the Fry farm.

By the fall of 1875, Sam Bass had cleaned up about all the loose racing money in northern Texas and had made an excursion into Indian Territory. Next he went to San Antonio and other points to the Southwest to bid for the Mexican cash. Here he put the Denton mare in the hands of a confederate, while he himself posed as a horse trainer and a judge of racing horses. On finding a horse he thought his could outrun, he would advise the owner to match it against Jenny. But even a racket as slick as this could not last long. Before many months, Sam sold his mare and embarked on the career that put him in the nation's headlines and led to his death at the hands of Texas Rangers.

By this time, quarter races already were being displaced in the larger centers by contests of greater length. But they persisted in the more remote communities and on the ranches. Sometimes they were found in Western Texas and in New Mexico in the early years of this century. They are still held in some rural sections below the Rio Grande.

AUTHORS INDEX
(Containing Original Title with Name and Date of Publication)

ANSON, WILLIAM

"Quarter-of-a-Mile Running Horses," originally appeared in *The Breeders Gazette,* August 24, 1922, entitled "About the Quarter Horse."

"The Oldest Distinct Breed," originally appeared in *The Breeders Gazette,* May 11, 18, 1910, entitled "Breeding a Rough Country Horse."

CASEMENT, DAN D.

"Concho Colonel, His Life and Times," originally appeared in *The American Hereford Journal,* June 1, 1927, entitled "Steel Dusts As I Have Known Them."

"The Social Significance," originally appeared in *The Cattleman,* September, 1940, entitled "The Social Significance of the Quarter Horse."

CASEMENT, JACK S.

"I Object," originally appeared in *Country Life,* October, 1939, entitled "Quarter Horses."

"Master of Two Trades," originally appeared in *The Western Livestock Journal,* October 15, 1940, entitled "Why We Stick to Steel Dusts."

"The Social Significance," originally appeared in *The Cattleman,* September, 1940, entitled "The Social Significance of the Quarter Horse."

CULLUM, GROVE

"I Do Not Like Him," originally appeared in *The Horse and Horseman,* May, 1939, entitled "The Quarter Horse."

"Importance of Racing and the Remount," originally appeared in *Polo,* June, 1935, entitled "The Western Horse."

DENHARDT, BOB

"Is the Quarter Horse a Thoroughbred," originally appeared in *The Cattleman*, March, 1940, under the same title.

"New Light on Old Steel Dust," originally appeared in *The Western Horseman*, November-December, 1939, under the same title.

"Peter McCue, Wonder Horse," originally appeared in *The Cattleman*, October, 1939, under the same title.

"Explanation For Speed," originally appeared in *The Horse*, May-June, 1939, entitled "Quarter Horse, An Explanation of His Speed."

"Short Horses," originally appeared in *The Western Horseman*, November-December, 1940, entitled "The Quarter Horse."

"Short-Horse" Men, original appearance.

"The South Texas Quarter Horse," originally appeared in *The Western Horseman*, March-April, 1940, entitled "The Billy Horse."

"The Quarter Horse, A History," to appear in *Country Life*, under the same title.

"The Southwestern Cow Horse," originally appeared in *The Cattleman*, April, 1939, under the same title.

DOBIE, J. FRANK

"Billy Horses and Steel Dust," originally appeared in *The Cattleman*, March, 1937, under the same title.

FLETCHER, H. T.

"He Was Called Billy," originally appeared in *The Breeders Gazette*, August 3, 1922, entitled "Quarter Horses in Texas."

GARD, WAYNE

"Losin' One's Shirt," originally appeared in *The Southwest Review*, July, 1940, entitled "The Quarter Horse."

HALL, J. GOODWIN

"The Colonial Quarter Horse," originally appeared in *The Cattleman*, September, 1941, entitled "The Quarter Horse and Quarter Racing."

HAND, ALBERT

"Worth His Salt," originally appeared in *The Horse Lover*, April, 1940, entitled "The Truth About Quarter Horses."

MOSES, GENE M.

"Cold Deck and Short Races," originally appeared in *The Remount*, September, 1924, entitled "The Quarter Horse."

MICHAELIS, HELEN

"The Great Little Horse Billy," originally appeared in *The Western Livestock Journal*, May 15, 1941, entitled "The Billy Horse."

"The Quarter Horse in Mexico," originally appeared in *The Cattleman*, September, 1940, under the same title.

GENERAL INDEX

Ace of Hearts, 25, 73-74, 89
Adams, Ott, 70, 103
Anson, William, xxi, 5-9, 51-53, 84, 89, 91-92, 113-14, 145, 150
Arabian, xxii, 130, 136, 208
Arch Oldham, 23, 70, 72, 112, 139-40
Association (American Quarter Horse), xxiii, 95, 135, 180, 217
Balleymooney, 19-20, 32, 93
Barney Owens, xx, 88-89, 138
Bass, Sam, 63, 223-25
Billy, horse xvi, 70, 75, 96-97; family 21-26, 65-76, 149
Blake, Coke, 53-56; horses, 53, 83
Blanton, Billy, 65, 70, 72, 140
Bob Wade, 90, 104

Bouldin, John, 99
Brown Jug, 5, 84
Burlingame, Milo, 56-59; picture, 71
Casement, Dan D., xv, xviii, 3, 73, 84, 148, 151, 204, 210
Casement, Jack S., xvi, xviii, 26, 44, 204; picture, 198
Clegg, George, xviii, 65, 71-72, 103
Cold Deck, xvii, 33-34, 53-54, 89
Colonial Q. H., 120-23, 143-44, 161-78
Concho Colonel, 6, 11-12, 32, 84
Conformation, xxiv, 5-6, 12-13, 28-29, 115, 117, 140, 180, 189-204, 215
Copper-Bottom, 83, 149
Cullum, Grove, xvii, xxii, 38, 56, 124, 146, 203

GENERAL INDEX *(Continued)*

Dan Tucker, xx, 77, 88-89, 138
Denhardt, Bob, xv, xix, xxiv, 51, 68, 76, 86, 135, 141, 152, 189, 196; picture, 198
Dexter, 95, 149
Dickson, Raymond, xviii, 75, 92-93
Dobie, J. Frank, xviii, 63
Families, 83, 147, 149
Faults, xvii-xviii, 203
Fleming, William, 22-23, 26, 70, 74, 96-97, 100-01
Fletcher, H. T., xv, 21
Frosty, 31, 151
Gard, Wayne, xxvi, 216
Gardner, Alex, 91, 101
Golden Chief, 95, 149
Hall, J. Goodwin, xxiii, 159
Hand, Albert, xxv, 210
Harmon Baker, 89, 93
Hutchins, Jack, xviii, 75, 92
Illinois, 138
Jim Ned, 5, 84, 92, 114
King, Frank, 80-81
Kleberg, Robt. J., xviii, 179
Little Joe, III, 25, 66-67, 70-72, 103
Little Joe (New Mexico), 18, 85
Little Steve, 15-16
Lobo, 72, 75, 92
Matthies, Fred, 96
McGonigle, George and Clay, vii, 74, 102
Mexico, xxiii, xxiv, 183, 185
Michaelis, Helen, xx, xxiii, 96, 181
Minnick, Jim, xviii, 80; picture, 198
Morgans, xxii, 80, 130, 146
Moses, Gene, xvii, 33
Origin of Q. H., 40, 109-11, 119-20, 126, 156, 159-80, 197, 218
Paisana, 65-66, 72, 97
Pancho (Gardner) 91-92, 102; (Warren) 72

Peter McCue, xx, 57-58, 86-95, 200; Breeding, 88-89; Descendants, 138; Racing Record, 89-90
Polo, 12, 16, 212-13
Prepotency, 12, 40, 85, 143
Racing, 35-36, 55-56, 99, 126, 159, 162, 216-26
Ranch Use, 4, 30-31, 115-18, 152, 204-15
Red Dog, 20, 32, 151
Remount Service, 87, 123, 129, 179
Roberds, Coke, xviii-xix, 90
Rondo, 26, 37-38, 66, 70, 71, 149-50
Roping, xvi, 24, 74, 195, 212
Senator, 11-12, 15
Sheeran, O. J., 65, 73
Sheley, Dow, 66, 71
Spanish horse, 76, 82, 157, 205-06; Influence on Q. H., 144, 160-61
Standard Bred, xxii, 130, 178
Steel Dust, xviii-xx, 1, 9-11, 54, 64, 69, 76-86, 97, 113, 220-22; pedigree, 77, 81; description, 82
Sykes, Crawford, 25-26, 66, 70-72, 103, 140
Texas horse, 76, 81-82
Texas A. and M., 118
Thoroughbred, xxi, 21, 37, 136-37; Quarter Horse influence, 111, 120, 126, 139, 145, 163-78, 202; cross breeding and registration, 75, 105, 112, 199, 202; faults, 203; Quarter Horse different, 193-204
Trammell and Newman, xx, 69, 88-90, 138
Triangle Bar, xvi, 4, 27, 151
Underwood, R. L. (Lee), xviii, xix, 95, 149; picture, 182
Watkins, Samuel, xx, 74, 138, 150
Warren, W. B. (Bill), xviii, 72, 94; picture, 198
Whalebone, 65-66, 72, 99
Yellow Wolf, 10, 66-67, 73, 101

www.ingramcontent.com/pod-product-compliance
Lightning Source LLC
Chambersburg PA
CBHW030310080526
44584CB00012B/510